D1060136

THE MOST OBLIGING MAN IN EUROPE

Life and Times of the Oxford Scout

CHRISTOPHER PLATT
with picture research by
CHARLOTTE WARD-PERKINS

London
GEORGE ALLEN & UNWIN
Sydney Boston Wellington

This book is dedicated to my friend Fred Wheatley, who served as scout's boy at Christ Church, staircase scout at The Queen's College and at Wadham, and finally, for thirty years, as Steward of St Antony's.

First published in Great Britain
by George Allen & Unwin
1986

George Allen & Unwin (Publishers) Ltd
40 Museum Street, London WC1A 1LU, UK

George Allen & Unwin (Publishers) Ltd
Park Lane, Hemel Hempstead, Herts HP2 4TE, UK

Allen & Unwin Inc.
8 Winchester Place. Winchester, MA 01890, USA

George Allen & Unwin Australia Pty Ltd
8 Napier Road, North Sydney, NSW 2060, Australia

George Allen & Unwin with the
Port Nicholson Press
PO Box 11-838 Wellington, New Zealand

ISBN 0 04 941017 2

Set in 12 on 14 pt Ehrhardt by Fotographics (Bedford) Ltd
and printed and bound in Great Britain by William Clowes Ltd, Beccles and London

CONTENTS

The Cut direct. or Oxford Etiquette!!

'And I wonder,' resumed Broome, 'what they take a scout and bedmaker to be?'

'I'll bet pints round,' said Dusterley, chuckling at his notion, 'they fancy him a hamphibious hanimal, – a cross between a harrand-boy and a chambermaid.'

'Well, gentlemen,' said I, 'I'm obliged by the hints you have given me; but I feel easy on that subject, as some of our old masters, who are scattered everywhere over the face of the globe, will readily explain these difficulties if referred to.'

Theodore Hook, ed., *Peter Priggins, the College Scout* (1841)

Fred Wheatley in action and enjoying every minute of it

"Cadders". Richard Cadman in his pantry — fifty years a scout at Trinity

INTRODUCTION

Memories, nostalgia, old friendships, lost youth . . . 'strong is the hold that Oxford lays upon men, and no less strange than strong'. It is a vision of

'Towery city and branchy between towers/Cuckoo-echoing, bell-swarmèd, lark-charmèd, rock racked, river rounded'

(Gerard Manley Hopkins, *Duns Scotus' Oxford*).

It brings back faces, the faces both of contemporaries long parted and of those who remained – the majestic, all-knowing Head Porter at the College Lodge, the Scouts on each staircase, the Buttery Man.

Some men thought of Cardinal Newman, Archbishop Temple, Matthew Arnold, John Keble; others, returning, looked out for their scouts. Dr Johnson was coldly received when he revisited his old College, Pembroke; Dr Radcliffe (the Master) would not even buy a copy of his *Dictionary*. Yet he was 'highly pleased' to find, still in College, all the servants he had known, and 'expressed great satisfaction at being recognised by them'. To John Betjeman it was the servants who set the standard for the College, 'more interesting and more efficient and human than the majority of the dons'. And who did the Colonial Governor ask for when he came up from his banana bog – who but Edward Miller, John Harris, William Peasley, Ted Vickers?

Scouts outlived them all. 'A mere don', in the reformed Oxford of the 1890s, complained that the happy class who enjoyed a secure and permanent residence in Oxford was limited almost entirely to Heads of Houses and College servants: scouts

A porter at St John's. Drawing by Muirhead-Bone

barely ever showed the 'outward and visible signs of advancing years', and perhaps it was they who were in fact the repositories of Oxford tradition. Richard Gunstone's Buttery at Magdalen was for thirty-four years the home of undergraduates; it was 'a landscape, a piece of architecture, a simple poem of England . . . in [Gunstone's] own voice was the sound of all the bells of England'. A Common Room Man at Corpus, Henry Coombes, came to the College as a scout's boy at the age of fourteen and retired after sixty-five years. Parts of some Colleges came to be known by the names of their servants – 'Gunner's', of course, the Buttery in Magdalen, described so fondly as 'Venner's' in *Sinister Street* ('this ripe old room, generous and dry as sherry wine'), or 'Bunce's Hall', the New Buildings at Corpus in the 1890s, which was then cared for by a Mr Bunce and his 'boy' Fred, known for the excellence of their whisky punch.

Colleges were so much smaller in those days. The Seniors at a teaching college like Pembroke, towards the end of the eighteenth century, consisted simply of the Master, the Viceregent, the Tutor, and two 'Lecturers in Hall'. At Exeter a century later only about eighty undergraduates were actually in residence, while Lincoln, even smaller, took fifty-five. Ten to twelve Fellows made a 'rather large' Governing Body in the 1890s, and as late as the early 1950s the typical, medium-sized College is described as providing a home for some 220 undergraduates, a Head of House, and fourteen Fellows.

Others existed entirely, or almost entirely, for their Fellows. At Cambridge, King's (near the end of the last century) took fewer than fifty undergraduates; but it had forty-seven Fellows, thirty in residence (of whom twenty-three lived in College). All Souls in Oxford had no students at all, undergraduates or graduates, and it still has none. In the early 1880s it and its endowments existed for the Warden (William Anson) and four 'permanent' resident Fellows in College, including a 'simple old clergyman', Dr Bertie, a kind of ancient monument. Dr Bertie's election dated back to 1837 when All Souls had existed for 'Founder's Kin', descended from the brothers of Archbishop Chichele – a privilege abolished only at the time of the Universities Act of 1856. Dr Bertie, brought

"Gunner"

The dull common room of Trinity dons, 1907

by two scouts to the table in a chair, was 'an awful warning against celibate old age spent in a couple of dreary rooms, with none but neglectful servants around'. In several other Colleges, said the historian Sir Charles Oman (elected to All Souls in the mid-1880s), there were similarly pathetic figures, including an old man in his own College, Cuthbert Shields, who was under the impression that he was a reincarnation of Zoroaster.

Long residence and tiny, claustrophobic numbers brought much unhappiness to what must have seemed, to most outsiders, a wonderfully privileged life. At the end of the eighteenth century the Tutor of St Catharine's (Cambridge) was lecturing on the Law of Extreme Necessity. Suppose, he said, he and the Master were struggling in the water for a plank which would hold only one, he (the Tutor) would be justified in knocking the Master off, adding, with great vehemence, 'Damn him – and I would do it too without the slightest hesitation!' Perhaps the loneliness, frustration and boredom of the Senior Common Room was at its worst in the late nineteenth century, when many Fellows had 'friends' outside (or, later, were actually married) and Fellow Commoners and noblemen were no longer admitted to the Common Room. It was certainly an atmosphere that bred eccentricity. Few of the Fellows before the reforms of the mid-nineteenth century had occupations; they stayed long enough only to secure a vacant College 'living'. Some went mad, like William Pugh, Fellow of Trinity (Cambridge) from 1790, who was finally detected creeping out of College at night and smashing street lamps, crying, 'You are Robespierre and you Danton, Saint-Just. . . .' Frederick Harrison describes an Oxford Common Room in the mid-nineteenth century where the Senior Tutor went on writing through the Bursar's twaddle, 'his fierce restless eye darting forth his deep-rooted hatred against the forms of social life – contempt for the Sub-Dean, scorn of the Bursar, loathing for the paralytic Fellow . . .'.

In all this, college scouts were the intermediaries. Lewis Carroll, a mathematics tutor, believed in the importance of degrading his pupils, in putting them in their place. He himself sat at the further end of the room. Outside the door (which was shut) sat the scout; outside the outer door (also shut) was the sub-scout; halfway downstairs sat the sub-sub-scout, and down in the yard sat the pupil. The lecture proceeded:

TUTOR: What is twice three?
SCOUT: What's a rice-tree?
SUB-SCOUT: When is ice free?
SUB-SUB-SCOUT: What is a nice fee?
PUPIL (timidly): Half a guinea?

The scout himself was brought much more closely in contact with his undergraduates in those days of hip baths, coal fires, oil lamps, meals in rooms and much entertaining. Real friendships developed, and at a time of bachelor Fellows, when dons were so much less capable of handling the social, physical and mental problems of the young, the scouts, family men of experience, made up for their deficiencies. It is probably true that scouts took more interest in sportsmen than in scholars: they even placed bets on them. Prowess in sport could be appreciated while they had no way of assessing scholarship. 'Sometimes they would say: "Well, he'll never pass his bloody exam, he hasn't done nothing", and that chap comes up with a First!'

No doubt there was too much of the tradition of servitude, too much of the abominable presumption upon service by which Roger Dataller, a former pit-man at working-class Ruskin College, meant the chatting-up by drunken undergraduates of cinema usherettes, the be-sir-ing that had nothing to do with ordinary politeness – a tradition of servitude that sapped the dignity of spirit of any full-grown man. Dataller listened (in 1929) to a servant of one of the Colleges describing the proceedings he had just seen: much drunkenness, smashed crockery and windows, sickness and excreta over the floors, valuable plants ripped from the gardens, tables, chairs and w.c. seats feeding bonfires, and filthy language. ' "I don't like it [he had said] and I've been in the Army at that. Them's the fellows you've got to call 'Sir'," and there was contempt in his eyes.' The Oxford of the 1920s, said another class-stranger, Goronwy Rees, was the creation (in many ways a beautiful one) of 'a highly developed class system'. It was not so unreasonable at the time. Benjamin Jowett, who had made Balliol the nursery of Britain's politicians and bureaucrats, agreed that one must expect to be accused of snobbishness if one tries to get hold of young men of rank and wealth, but then it is worth remembering that it makes sense to influence towards good those who are going themselves to have influence over the lives of hundreds or thousands.

Anyway, Gentlemen Commoners were known and distinguished as 'Tufts' by the gold tassels on their mortar boards. Urquhart of Balliol liked people to be well-born, and if possible Roman Catholic; 'Sligger's' Savoyard chalet housed reading parties that included the young Harold Macmillan, while no place was found for the common man.

The Privileged: undergraduate members of the Phoenix Club, c 1900

Students washing up in working class Ruskin, 1906

Lyttelton Gell, Conservative candidate for Oxford in the General Election of 1892 and attached in some way to Balliol, lived in state on Headington Hill. He and his well-connected wife were at home to Balliol men on Sundays: the first Sunday of Term to members of the aristocracy, the second to sons of gentlemen and the third to Americans and Jews. Christ Church, itself the home of privilege, was internally divided. The best people even in the 1920s were in Tom Quad, and they did not talk to anyone else at all; they accepted that others, the Lords and Earls, lived in Canterbury and that it was possible to doss down in Peckwater: the Meadow Buildings were there but never acknowledged. Only Harold Acton, an aesthete, actually *preferred* the Buildings, painting his rooms yellow and filling them with Victorian bric-à-brac: 'back to mahogany was [his] battle cry'. It could be the most unpleasant of atmospheres, provoking to the rebel. Max Beerbohm had once been a modest, good-humoured boy: it was Oxford, he said, that had made him insufferable.

Ranking was as furious within classes as between them. Tradespeople would not associate with servants, even at a village dance. In a great house before the First World War, where there might be as many twenty servants, the lady's maid would lose caste if seen walking out with the kitchen-maid and the cook could not be found talking with

MR. ROBERT FILCHER BRINGS SUPPLIES FROM THE BUTTERY.

Servants in Hall, Merton, 1923

the second footman. It was not always sensible, or kind, to react against it. In the depressed 1930s a rich young American, Michael Straight (a radical fellow-traveller at the time), told his Cambridge servant that he could keep him no longer. Was he asking too much (four dollars a week)? No, said Straight, he just did not believe in being waited on. 'But sir,' said his gentleman's gentleman, 'if young gentlemen like you don't employ us, what's to become of us?' Straight did not know the answer and neither did the undergraduates at the Queen's College (Oxford). The radical chic at Queen's in the Depression insisted on personally standing their scouts an entitlement of a weekly pint in the Buttery; the less socially-minded gave a token to the grateful scout to be spent across the street on groceries for his hungry family off the Iffley Road.

Scouts were conservatives. They liked to see wine flow rather than cocoa; they preferred, said Betjeman, to see a young man stupefied with his first experience of mixed drinks rather than exhilarated by his first reading of *Das Kapital.* Scouts were 'all just regular lower-middle, upper-working class Tory, you know . . . just easy going, placid types'.

Chapter 1

SERVANTS IN COLLEGE

Scouts were a part of Collegiate life. Although College servants have existed, in one form or another, as long as the Colleges themselves, the period for which the profession of scout survived was relatively short. Scouts were personal servants employed directly by Oxford Colleges for the care of each 'staircase', for it was up and down staircases (eight to ten 'sets' on each), rather than along corridors, that College accommodation was traditionally arranged.

A scullion at Christ Church in the late seventeenth century, the earliest painted portrait of a college servant

The butler at Oriel holding the Founder's Cup, an early nineteenth century engraving

In fact it was only from the early decades of the nineteenth century that service by scouts took its now familiar form, and by the 1970s the institution had almost vanished. There is no uniformity between Colleges, and much overlap. Although the term 'scout' to describe a personal, male servant was known by the eighteenth century, the employment of servants was the responsibility of the young men themselves. The majority of the 'students', as Gentlemen Commoners, were in any case hardly more than paying guests, receiving no disciplined education whatever and taking nothing from the Colleges other than a daily dinner in Hall; basic accommodation was supplied by the Colleges, to be furnished and maintained by the undergraduates. Just as they had in Eton, the new Gentlemen Commoners brought with them their personal servants – boy grooms and footmen, sometimes known as 'tigers'. Theodore Hook, the waggish don who wrote *Peter Priggins* (pseudo-memoir of an Oxford scout), invented a Byron Montgomery Jilks who brought his aunt's servant Timothy with him to Oxford in the 1840s. It is an indication of the times that by now there was a male 'bedmaker' provided by the College, and Timothy had little to do other than keep his master supplied with cigars and himself with 'baccy'.

For the rich, little changed right up to the Second World War. Even in the 1930s wealthy undergraduates took their gentleman's gentleman with them to civilise their digs, although, in College, 'scouts' (Oxford) and 'gyps' (Cambridge) by now provided full services. While it was still dark, Michael Straight's manservant stepped silently into the bedroom of his master's Cambridge digs. He would pour a jug of water into a bowl for a wash and shave. He would put out Straight's socks, his shirt and his student's gown, and assign the tie that he felt appropriate. Then, in a low and deferential voice he would announce that it was time to rise and, once a week, enquire whether he should 'draw' a bath.

In fact, in Cambridge, residence in College was never so widely and universally practised as at Oxford; about a third of Cambridge undergraduates were living in approved lodgings until the last quarter of the nineteenth century. The ancient

The Cambridge Gyp from E Bradley COLLEGE LIFE, *1850*

universities have changed much over the centuries. In late medieval times, in a foundation like New College, it was the choristers who made the beds and provided the domestic services, although other servants were employed besides. Women servants, as in all medieval statutes, were debarred, and even the 'latrix', working at her linen outside the College, had to be of 'such age and condition that no sinister suspicion can, or ought to follow her'. In medieval Corpus Christi, the Fellows and Scholars slept one of each to every room, the Fellow in the high bed and the Scholar on a truckle near by; the Fellow supervised the Scholar, while the Scholar made the beds and kept the room in order.

In practice, Colleges must all have maintained at least a core of their own servants, for the Kitchen and the Lodge, for the clearing and maintenance of buildings, quadrangles and courts, and for delegated tasks like laundry beyond the College gate. In the days of pigtails, wigs and powdered hair, when the young gentlemen were

A chorister carrying food and drink, from a medieval carving over the Buttery door, New College

Cambridge servants: engraving from COLLEGE LIFE *(left) and Trinity bedmakers and porters, 1884 (above)*

expected to have their hair dressed every day, College servants usually included a barber.

Yet, apart from that core, it was quite common for the Colleges' higher servants to be taken from the 'reduced' gentry; the stigma of service was a development of the eighteenth century and after.

'Servitors' at Oxford ('sizars' at Cambridge) were the younger brothers of pensioners, the sons of clergymen 'poor as a sod of smouldering coal'; it was an avenue to education that came to be closed, from the mid-eighteenth century, by a new and demanding upper-bourgeoisie. Isaac Newton was a sub-sizar in Trinity, Cambridge, the philosopher Richard Bentley a sub-sizar at St John's, and they shared their position with several distinguished members of the episcopal bench. John Prideaux DD, Lord Bishop of Worcester in the seventeenth century, started right at the bottom as a scullery boy, but his case, so frequently cited, was quite clearly exceptional.

When, ultimately, their own distinct profession emerged, scouts were only one of the categories of College servants, although the most numerous, and the vocabulary is complicated by the different meanings employed between College and College, University and University. At both Oxford and Cambridge the class of personal servant paid by the College was at its highest point in the nineteenth century, when 'gyps' and 'scouts' – men servants all – performed and directed the main duties, assisted by 'bedmakers', helps and underscouts. In Cambridge the work passed to women rather earlier than it did at Oxford and 'bedmakers', once of either sex but now exclusively women, assumed the main functions of the 'gyp'. At Oxford the reverse occurred, and male 'scouts', assisted by male 'underscouts' or 'boys', took over the role of their female assistants and in turn were rationalised out of existence after the Second World War. In some Colleges, the employment of women servants had always been positively prohibited, although perhaps in most, even the more traditional, women found employment below the stairs; 'part-time women' were cheapest.

No proper ladder existed within College service, where jobs and departments were so

A staircase scout and his "sets", New College 1890

different one from another. The Head Porter, in charge of his own department (the College 'Lodge'), was probably the senior. Compton Mackenzie remembered the 'unctuous tones of Kingston', the majestic porter at Magdalen in the early 1900s, and in Balliol the smile of welcome from Hancock, who was 'surely the most obliging man in Europe'. 'Fred of Oxford' certainly thought of himself, with his staff of under-porters and night porter, as directly responsible simply to the Master. The Manciple, for those Colleges that employed such people, was in overall control of catering. Next came the Senior Common Room Man. The Master's Lodge was a separate department, served by its own staff. The Buttery Scout, again running a small department of his own, was just above the rest and paid slightly more in recognition. The post of Senior Scout, on the other hand, meant very little in small Colleges, where its holder was simpy longest on the job, acting mainly as a mouthpiece for scouts and as a channel for instructions (although in a bigger College expected to take some part in occasional recruitment).

The scouts themselves were assisted by underscouts or scouts' boys (subcontracted often by themselves until after the Great War). Women (if any), kitchen hands and messengers came last. Messengers, fresh from Board School, were charged, until comparatively recently, with the task of bringing around the mail several times a day, and they might be asked (and paid) to polish boots and even to buy theatre tickets besides; before the First World War Colleges rarely had their own Junior Common Room and never telephones, so that the young men lived, worked and played in their own rooms, sending written notes to each other two or three times a day.

College service was recognisably a hierarchy, although distinctions and differences of wages were often slight. Each College was different and much – sometimes all – depended on personality. But the various departments of the College remained very independent of one another. The hierarchy at Corpus Christi, for example, ran thus right into the 1960s: Bursary, Lodge, Kitchen, Buttery, Senior Common Room, Staircases (scouts), Furnaces and, finally, Gardens. And this was where scouts, unambitious men, were often happy to remain.

Two servants from Merton. Joseph Chamberlain (left), clerk in the Lower Bursary 1868-1907. Charles Patey (right) started work in 1836, aged seven, opening the Hall door to assist his father who was Common Room man (and gave his name to Patey's Quad). He succeeded his father and was appointed Butler in 1869, in which post he remained until his death in 1916 after seventy eight years service

Chapter 2

SHIFTING HOURS

Scouts were not long at Oxford and the pattern of College life has changed much both before and since. In any case, Colleges have never entirely reflected contemporary custom. The hour of dinner in New College, in the third quarter of the last century, was determined simply by the Fellows' wish to change for dinner after Chapel (at 5 p.m.), so that Hall took place at 6.15 – early even by the standards of half a century before. Nowadays, Colleges dine around 7.15, in part to spare kitchen staff, but as much to provide undergraduates with a full evening for entertainment. Again, the hour is early by modern standards, but who at Oxford has ever cared a jot for that?

Nonetheless, the tendency over the centuries has been to start the day later and end it later. In pre-Reformation Cambridge, dinner (the principal meal of the day) was as early as 10 a.m., and supper at 5 p.m. Indeed, in the sixteenth century the general hour of rising was 5 a.m. All Colleges opened their gates at this hour and closed them again in winter at 8 p.m. and at 9 in summer. Two centuries later, although mornings began later, the evening hours remained much the same; they were recorded, in fact, in the Laudian statutes by which scholars were expected to return to their Colleges before nine o'clock when a curfew was proclaimed by the great bell at Christ Church.

But change was on its way – what a President of Caius called 'the well-known secular drift onwards of the dinner hour'. Early in the eighteenth century the Colleges went to dinner at twelve and to supper at six and over the century dinner moved further to 1.30 or 2 p.m. At 8 p.m. 'all supped on broiled bones and beer', after which the dons gathered at some adjoining tavern or coffee house. Tom's Coffee House in the High Street was a

Engraving by Robert Cruikshank from THE ENGLISH SPY, *1827*

favourite with both dons and undergraduates, the undergraduates drinking and smoking in the front room and in the large room upstairs, while the older men, the choice spirits of the University, met in a small inner apartment on the ground floor ('the House of Lords') where they also smoked their pipes and drank beer and wine; 'drunkenness was unquestionably, at the time, the prevailing vice of Oxford'. The 'smart' in early eighteenth-century Oxford (those known as 'fops' to the nineteenth century) spent between 10 a.m. and 11 a.m. at Lyne's coffee house, took a turn or two in the Meadow under Merton wall while the dullards were dining in the College hall (shortly after mid-day), dined privately in their rooms at one, spent the afternoon (after dressing carefully) in one of the coffee houses, went to Chapel, and then drank tea with some celebrated beauty.

A contrast has traditionally been drawn between beer and talk at Cambridge and, at Oxford, wine and conversation. Cambridge dons in the eighteenth century, after dining in Hall at 1 p.m., drank Madeira and port in the Combination Room until 4 p.m., went to the coffee house and to their daily paper at 5 p.m., had supper back in the Combination Room at 7 p.m., and spent the rest of the evening drinking and playing cards. Fellows at Oxford dined also at 1 p.m., but they conversed and drank wine until tea at 5.30, after which there was music – harpsichord, flute and viols – accompanied by punch and lemonade, until supper was brought by the servants at 9.30 p.m. Once the supper cloth was removed, some drank negus and others hot egg flip, while still others sang catch and glee. The party at Oxford dissolved at 11 p.m., when the guests returned home to their Colleges, and the hosts went to bed.

No doubt the account is idealised. In the course of the eighteenth century the traditional dinner time of between twelve and one o'clock came at some Colleges to what was felt to be the extraordinarily late hour of 3 p.m., after which there was port and dessert in the afternoon, Chapel for the few at 5 p.m., and tea for those who were not too drunk to take it at 6 p.m. Undergraduates then settled into an evening of 'dull and hard drinking, frivolous gossip and Boeotian uproar':

At nine, the blinking Scout appears
While most are nodding in their chairs,
And bottles moves away,
For from the Kitchen he has brought
What each one sober might or ought
Have order'd on his tray:
Boil'd fowl, salt herrings, sausages,
Cold beef and brawn and bread and cheese
With tankards full of ale.

Dinner by the 1820s had advanced to four and then to five in the afternoon. Winstanley reported that in the early 1860s some seniors in Cambridge were asking for their main meal at 6.30 p.m., while the undergraduates still dined at four or five. However, the pressure was to increase the length of the afternoon so as to allow time for modern recreation; dinner, in the late nineteenth century, had reached its modern hour with Colleges dining regularly at 7 p.m. In some Colleges, Hall came, as in King's before the First World War, at 7.15 precisely, a compromise between high tea and supper.

England is a land of snobbery and class distinction, where all innuendoes are observed. *Cosi fan tutte.* Christ Church dined at 7.30 in the 1930s, while plebeian Queen's went to Hall at 7.15. 'Queen's was a step down, rather, you know', said Fred Wheatley, 'they were ordinary people at Queen's.' And Queen's, we all know, was the land of 'a cugger of cocoa, a sigger-sogger round the piano'.

Grand dinner in the new dining hall, Balliol, 1877

BLACK MATINS, or the Effect of Late drinking upon Early Risers.

From THE ENGLISH SPY

Chapter 3

MORNING

Morning, for the Victorians, began later than it had for Tudors and Stuarts. Undergraduates were rising as late as they dared for a dash to Chapel at 8 a.m., pyjamas concealed (they hoped) under a loose layer of outer clothing. The scouts themselves and their assistants had been at work since 6 a.m., emptying slops, removing the ashes, bringing up the coal and lighting the fires, cleaning the outer room and tidying up after the night before.

Undergraduate rooms, a set that consisted of a generous sitting room ('sitter') and poky, cold bedroom ('bedder'), were masculine and austere – on the walls reproductions of Primavera, the Mona Lisa, Mantegna's 'St George', Watts's 'Sir Galahad', 'The Soul's Awakening' and perhaps two 'cattle subjects'. Sportsmen kept to their prints and Dr Grundy once found an undergraduate friend, on the eve of a visit from his 'black Protestant' father, removing the sporting prints from his wall; he was substituting a number of old woodcuts of subjects from the Old Testament, hired for the day from Ryman's (the picture dealer in the High).

Girl undergraduates lived more simply in bed-sitters, with walls green and cream, convertible divans and gas stoves: they drank cocoa and kia-ora, and were fed on warm cutlets and gravy off cold plates at a long table decked with daffodils. Like Dorothy Sayers and her heroine Harriet Vane, they sat talking late, gas fires glowing, over their coffee and parkin. It was a wholly innocent world of 'hot drinks and woolly dressing gowns, purest Somerville'.

Standards were sometimes higher. An aesthete like Stephen Spender hung reproduc-

"Warm cutlets and gravy off cold plates at a long table decked with daffodils". The first dining hall in Lady Margaret Hall, c 1890

A bedsitter at Somerville, 1880

Undergraduates at LMH, 1888, presided over by the Principal, Elizabeth Wordsworth, one of the psychic pair who saw Marie Antoinette in the Trianon Gardens. Gertrude Bell shows a haughty profile in the centre row

tions of Gauguin, Van Gogh and Paul Klee on his walls; it was not what Cousin Jasper would have approved, and Compton Mackenie's Honourable Lonsdale behaved more characteristically when he simply transplanted his study at Eton to Oxford. 'Young men', said James Pycroft (*Oxford Memoirs*, 1886), 'who are fond of feathers, fans and crockery, had perhaps better seek some other place than an Oxford College for the gratification of their peculiar tastes.'

It was the scouts' job to cope with them all. Long after the appearance of gas, coal fires were still the main form of heating in the Colleges. Scouts built these up to a fierce heat: nobody can say how Colleges survived – probably, said George Saintsbury, because it seemed impossible that they should. But heaped fires were an Oxford custom. In the Union they burned like the furnaces of a railway engine; Victor Gollancz saw great bucketsful of coal flung on roaring fires by the attendants, and when you thought they had finished they had only just begun.

LITTLE MR. BOUNCER'S BREAKFAST.

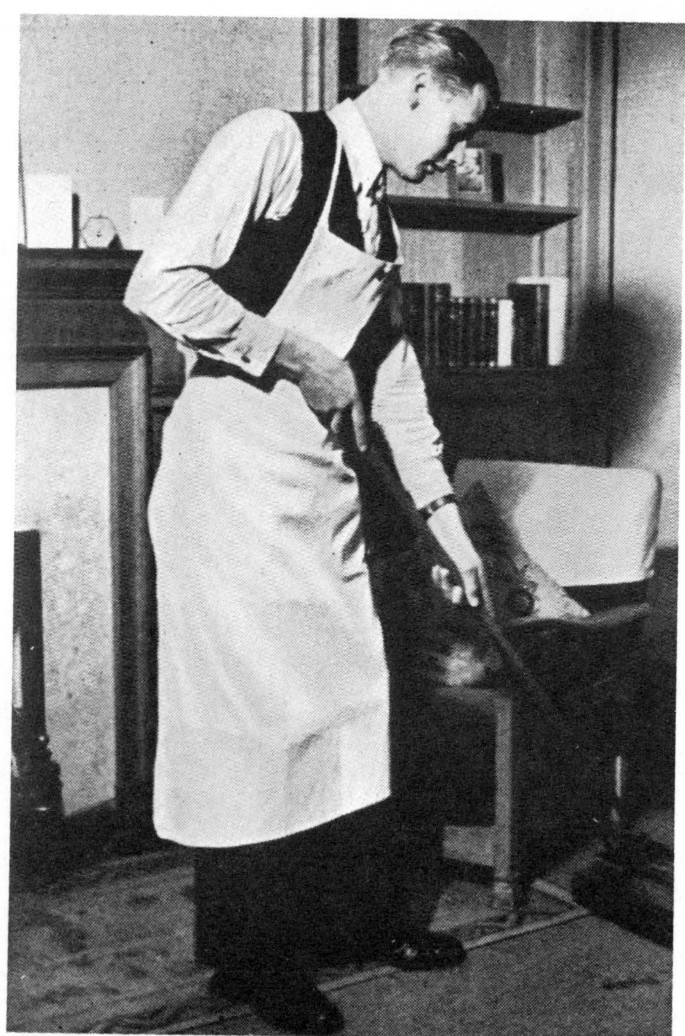

Scouts at work

A scout and his boy in a College like Christ Church, where an undergraduate might expect fires both in his study and in his sitting room (nobody in those days gave a thought to heat in bedrooms) might have been responsible for keeping up to twelve of these fires cleaned, lit and burning. In a smaller College, where the scout worked on his own, he kept at least eight. The burden was considerable. The carrying of coals in the great houses before 1914 was the heaviest labour of the otherwise underworked footmen. Some abbeys and castles kept upward of sixty fires alight, and many burned more than a ton of coal a day.

Carting coal, clearing, laying and lighting fires, was heavy work enough in Colleges, but then there was breakfast. Scouts summoned their undergraduates at 7.30 a.m. with hot water and orders for breakfast. 'Tampson', one Merton don called angrily to his scout, 'do not, I beg, let this occur again; you have given me an undergraduate's egg!' And undergraduates, until after the Second World War, took their breakfast in their rooms, except in New College (where breakfast was served in the Junior Common Room) and in Keble (where breakfast, supplied economically in Hall, was 'eating bacon-and-eggs and talking about bishops'). The most modest were those thrifty undergraduates who took a breakfast of porridge and a 'commons' of loaf, butter and marmalade. Life was better for athletes in training who, after their morning run, were fed on fish, chops or steaks. 'Ordinary men', in Tom Brown's day (1850s), were content with buttered toast and eggs, with a dish of broiled ham, marmalade and bitter ale. Grandees at 'the House' (Christ Church) might order stewed kidneys, underdone beef steaks, plovers' eggs (in season), potted game, cold ham, Wytham strawberries, a dainty omelette, twists of rolls from a distant baker, dove tarts (pigeon pie), spread-eagles (grilled pressed fowl, rolled with butter, sprinkled with pepper and served with mushroom sauce), and quart silver tankards of pale ale or brown stout (with tea and coffee held in reserve).

It was not always to be so. When herrings were suggested for the breakfast menu at King's in the 1930s the ancient bursar cried out in his high-pitched voice: 'Luxury,

The room of a sporting Magdalen undergraduate at 135 High Street, c 1890

Housing the poor, Ruskin, 1939

St John's, 1875

luxury! I shall vote against it!' But in May-time, oh, the dim still mornings with the 'sitter' casements opened on the limes and elms, bacon and ambrosial coffee, 'curled upon the window seat – ourself and our best pal... *Carpe diem, Carpe diem*!'

Breakfast parties among undergraduates were a favourite occasion, proverbial in Victorian Oxford, finishing sentimentally with a loving cup, or, more mundanely, with a tankard of beer iced or mulled to season. By the end of the century greater pressures, and less time, meant that breakfast parties gradually gave way to luncheons. But Victor Gollancz, as an undergraduate at New College just before the First World War, was asked at the right season to as many as three breakfasts in the same morning – kedgeree and large flattish omelettes with hot tomato sauce – and he made a point of going to them all. Sunday breakfast was less sociable, taken late at the shop opposite Balliol with a few solitary men from Balliol and Trinity, in bedroom slippers. They looked up as Charles Ryder entered and then turned back to their newspapers. Everybody else was dressed for church, apart from 'four proud infidels', Indians from Balliol, on their way to the river in snow-white turbans, freshly laundered white flannels and neatly pressed blazers, a picnic basket, and Shaw's *Plays, Pleasant and Unpleasant.*

Later, on a weekday, when breakfast was over, undergraduates went to their lectures and scouts were left to clear up – College kitchens took charge of the washing up of college property and the scouts simply ferried the débris, yet many undergraduates in those days used to bring their own crockery, linen, glass and silver, and no sooner had breakfast been cleared from the table, washed up and put away, than it seemed time to lay for lunch. Normally, however, at 10.30 or 11.00 the scouts went home on their bicycles to East and South Oxford, and to Jericho.

Undergraduates have always liked to give the impression that they do no work at all, and this is often true. Some *did* work. In any case, lectures and tutorials never started before ten o'clock so that there was plenty of time for a leisurely breakfast before Schools. Others found lectures detestable. The young Shelley, after rushing enthusiastically to his first lecture (in geology), was asked what it was like: 'Oh it was about

Merton kitchens before improvements in 1961

stones, stones, stones. . . .' But relatively few men went to lectures, the usefulness of which (as Christopher Hobhouse explained) had been superseded some while ago by the invention of the printing press.

About 12.15 the scouts were back again. In most Colleges before the Second World War, undergraduates were still served lunch in their own rooms and only dinner was taken in Hall. Queen's was an exception from as early as the 1930s since so many of its undergraduates lived out of College in digs and lunch had to be provided communally. 'Commons' at lunch was an extension of breakfast – a simple plate of bread and cheese, and a pint of ale in a silver tankard. But the ordinary lunch, just slightly above the primitive, might consist of a cold chicken leg, bread, cheese and ale, served by a scout in each set of rooms. Kitchen porters in Christ Church, with trays on their heads, moved

FIRST SCOUT *(referring to fellow scout who has just passed)*: Wot's hup with 'Erbert to-day? 'E's gort swelled 'ead, 'e 'as.

SECOND SCOUT: 'Aven't you 'eard? The proctor mistook 'im for a Vawsity genelman last night.

around the College from staircase to staircase. The young bloods could order lunch à la carte, or take a 'club lunch', a three-course set lunch sent to their rooms. But most undergraduates by the inter-war period took only commons – cheese and bread rolls, or what was left of a quarter of a cottage loaf, enlivened by a tin of sardines or by some slices of salami. College lunches in the 1920s and 1930s were no occasion, and demand was modest.

Fred Wheatley describes serving lunch for two old bachelor dons at Queen's ('Quaggers' to an earlier generation) just before the Second World War. It was a chilly day in September with the table moved up to the hearth, a simple meal of cold duck, salad, cheeses and fruit (no pudding); the table was laid up with two bottles of white wine (one Chablis and the other Meursault) and two clarets. At 5.30 p.m., after tea time, Fred removed what remained to an accompanying chorus of snores.

Chapter 4

AFTERNOON

It is the Oxford afternoon that evokes the most powerful nostalgia. Scouts had little part in it, since they were off duty and at home most afternoons from around 2.30 – unless they had a hunting man on their staircase and had to be on hand to pull off his boots. Meanwhile their more elderly masters walked or snoozed while the 'young barbarians were out at play'. Nobody in the University, apart from those improbable scientists, remained indoors:

> *Here coming rulers, who will one day wield*
> *Old empire's rod, our England's finest flower,*
> *Practise their prentice-hand in mimic strife,*
> *And playing field,*
> *Learning the Master's touch and Maker's life.*
>
> (Frederick William Ward, *Oxford the Dreamer*)

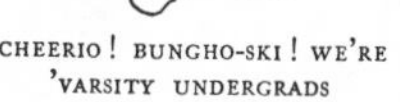

CHEERIO! BUNGHO-SKI! WE'RE 'VARSITY UNDERGRADS

Organised games were the hideous product of an imperial century. Walking, for the majority of undergraduates, had once been the sole form of exercise. Only for the few was there a little cricket in May, some hunting and shooting, fencing and riding, horse jumping, tandem driving, a little boating, but no fives as yet, tennis or croquet, and hockey and football were left to young boys. No ordinary reading man, said the President of Caius, ever did anything in the afternoon other than walk in the country. Even the aesthetes went out for little walks.

The country, in those days, was not far from the Colleges. At two o'clock, in pairs and

Undergraduates at play, Worcester, 1880

The Lime Walk, Trinity

From COLLEGE LIFE

Off to the Races, Magdalen, 1912

threes, the whole of Oxford University was out for an eight to ten mile walk up the Iffley, Headington, Banbury and Woodstock Roads. Oxford was not yet surrounded by a suburban fringe, and to the north, south and west the Rev. Tuckwell described the city as cut short 'clear as a walled and gated Jericho'.

This was in the 1830s, and Park Town, built in 1854, anticipated the suburban growth of red-brick North Oxford (from the 1860s) by at least a decade, E. C. Carrit, a don for the first half of the twentieth century, described Oxford in his undergraduate days as still just a country town, where droves of cattle jostled through the streets and his bicycle once rebounded from a sow in the Broad. The formidable Mark Pattison was out for three to five hours a day, walking regularly with don and undergraduate alike. Like Benjamin Jowett, Pattison kept silent throughout. 'The irony of Sophocles', said one desperate freshmen, 'is greater than the irony of Euripides.' Pattison gave him a sour look and said nothing; they trudged on to Iffley. As they turned, Pattison opened his mouth: 'Quote', he said. Launcelot Phelps, Fellow and later Provost of Oriel, flowing beard under speckled straw hat, went striding across the fields with a band of undergraduates following *non passibus aequis.* The Fellows of All Souls, in a Sunday pack, walked regularly to Beckley. But then everyone did. One well-authenticated Spooner story tells of the occasion when he, like others, was out with a friend walking in North Oxford. They met a widow lady dressed in black to whom the Warden raised his hat. When she had passed, he turned sadly to his friend: 'Poor soul, very sad – eaten by missionaries – poor soul!'

Carrit himself took twenty-mile walks on Sundays, the 'Sunday grind', accompanied by Phelps. They would lunch at some favourite inn, Beckley, Brill or Stanton Harcourt, or with friends at Studley Priory. Others marched up to the Berkshire Downs, and when bicycles reached Oxford in the 1890s the idea of heaven as expressed by one don (who had taken to the bicycle late in life) was riding down Boar's Hill with his feet on the handlebars and the view of Oxford ahead.

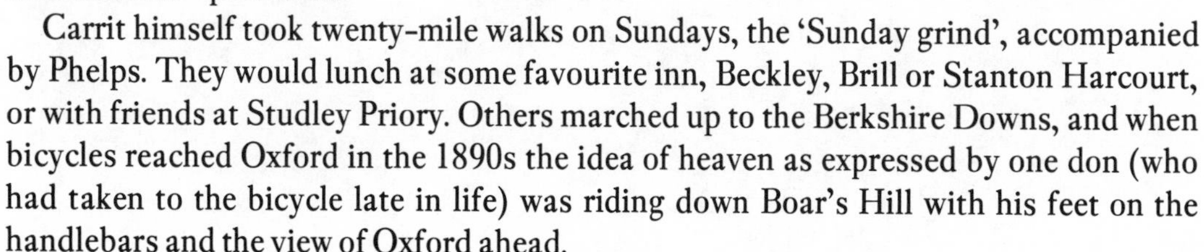

In early days before organised boat clubs and disciplined eights, boating had quite

Soccer team, Hertford, 1885

The "Rudolph Ramblers", Magdalen, 1912

different charms. On Isis 'embower'd amid thy willow trees. . . . Oft on the stream I've caught the breeze/And trimm'd the swelling sail'. In the seventeenth century an undergraduate took his love to Medley where boatmen stood ready –

And cream and cakes and pruines too,
But now alas she's left me,
Falero, lero, loo.

But even organised rowing became a popular pastime, most probably, as Noel Annan explains, because it gave the otherwise physically inept what they wanted but could not obtain from games in any other way – physical exhaustion, a sense of achievement and camaraderie. Leslie Stephen, when a don at Trinity, is described by Annan as having a place among the great rowing coaches of Victorian Cambridge; it was thus that he could overcome his intellectuality and feel himself at one with those 'manly affectionate fellows' he had admired as an undergraduate at Trinity Hall.

St Hilda's, the wrong side of Magdalen Bridge, 1880

Parsons' Pleasure, 1894. The pose is right but the bathing suit is an afterthought

In the days before Oxford's new drainage scheme and purified water, boating remained far less delightful than it has since become. Queen Victoria once asked, when standing on a Cambridge bridge, what all those bits of paper signified, to which the Master replied, with great presence of mind, 'Madame, those are notices prohibiting bathing.' But bathing became a passion in the ancient universities and naked dons plunged from green grass into the Cam and from Parson's Pleasure into the Cherwell: there in Cambridge was portly Oscar Browning, Secretary of the Cambridge Swimming Club, frisking quite naked with his companions, while in Oxford Hilaire Belloc bathed with his Balliol friends in winter rivers, wrestling together under the sun. 'Emeritus', in the *Oxford Magazine* of 1906, recalled the healthy fun of youth:

Mind'st thou that frog we put in Harry's stocking?
Harry, as he went a'swimming,
Where the may-fly all were skimming,
Till he landed, mother-naked in the hospitable hay:
Does he mind it now, I wonder, District-judging in Bombay?

Oxford, after the Reforms, played hard. The 'new dons' wanted work from every undergraduate, but it was the man who read hard, rowed hard and, best of all, did *both* who won most respect. Dr Grundy's autobiography (*Fifty-five years at Oxford*, 1945) called attention to a cult of the body as powerful as that of the soul; a man who did not keep his body as fit as he might was sinning against Nature – he was not using that physical life on earth that God had given him. The most successful of his students, Grundy explained, were those who had represented the College on the river, in cricket, rugby or football.

Games were invented by Victorian public schools to keep the young out of mischief. The same strategy was applied quite naturally by Colleges, where the problem for young men, bored and repelled by rote-learning of remote classics, was to exhaust their energy on the river and dispel, with 'harmonic evenings' and debate, the drunken

The Oxford Gymnasium, 1859

bestiality of the eighteenth century. Leslie Stephen's cult of athleticism, Noel Annan explains, was 'a palliative for the recurrent disease of student boredom' – what one Cambridge don described as 'pestilent muscular Christianity'.

Games took their toll. As soon as the weather improved Mark Pattison found his undergraduates totally preoccupied with their preparations for play, playing itself, or recovering from their exertions. Christ Church's young aristocrats were 'either the foppish exquisite of the drawing room, or the barbarised athlete of the arena'; Brasenose by the late nineteenth century was already known for its prowess in sport and 'eminent as a College for Pass men'; most Colleges, by now, were only half a mile from their own sports grounds, and the University Parks were but a mile to the north.

It was fortunate that not every undergraduate turned to sport and that the Oxford walk survived. Michael Fane (*Sinister Street*) took his long afternoon walks through the silent Oxford countryside with his co-tenant Alan – and this was at the end of the

"Buttered toast and tea things gleaming in the firelight". Lincoln, c 1900

A winter walk under the elms. Broad Walk, 1880

century, long after the crushing victory of competitive games. Fane came home to his digs late in the afternoon where he found buttered toast and tea-things glimmering in the firelight; he and Alan then smoked the second best pipe of the day. It was an advantage of life in digs that landladies so often supplied the tea, when College undergraduates bought their own; crumpets, toasted teacakes, honey buns, anchovy toast and Fuller's walnut cake. Or there was tea at the Buttery, and 'hotters' ordered from the kitchen.

Scouts returned between five and five-thirty, when they lit the gas jets on the staircases, stoked up the fires, drew the curtains and cleared the tea-things. Such freedom and independence from adult control was something that none of these young men had known – no bell after tea to summon them to prep, nothing to prevent a visit to friends in another College, a stroll over to the Union with its deep armchairs and thick tobacco smoke, or even a couple of hours' work before dinner in Hall.

Tea, that Oxford occasion, had not existed before the 1880s, possibly because an Oxford dinner, then at 6 p.m., left too short an afternoon; Charles Oman reported that in his undergraduate days a caller was given not tea but a glass of sherry or claret and a slice or two of cake: 'there were always solid plum cakes in our cupboards.'

But Hall by now was at 7.15 and there was time even for books – unless the company was too good, the conversation too long, the fire too bright and the bath too warm.

"The governor writes that you'd like me to put you up to the ways of the place."

Dessert in Magdalen JCR, 1890

Chapter 5

EVENING

The curtains were drawn, tea was cleared, the fire built up to a fierce heat: time for the young gentlemen's bath. Baths were not always to be had so late in the day but an evening bath was much pleasanter, for

Chilly is the path –
Most chilly and most drear –
That lies 'twixt bed and bath
O Chilly is the path!

A tradition of cold baths – the Honest British Cold Bath – was long established. The President's Lodge at Corpus, Victorian, was built without a bathroom, and the President was himself content with a can of cold water in his bedroom. Lancelot Phelps of Oriel took a cold bath in his bedroom every day of his long life; on a frosty morning he could be heard muttering to himself: 'Be a man, Lancelot, be a man.'

Oxford Colleges had no plumbed baths of their own until the end of the last century; one Head of House could not understand the need since, as he said, the young men were up for no more than eight weeks at a time. The College baths at King's in 1909 were the first in Cambridge, and among the Fellows only Oscar Browning had his own bathroom – it was in this that Leo Maxse had once succeeded in locking him, snob that he was, with the Duke of Clarence (the Heir Presumptive).

College baths, even by the 1930s, were singularly uninviting. Undergraduates crossed Whewell's Court (Trinity) in dressing gowns and slippers, carrying a towel and a bar of soap; they went down into a dark catacomb, felt their way over the slippery floor of the showers, then turned on a tap and jumped up and down under a stream of cold water. Michael Straight told his horrified mother (American) that he had not had a bath for three weeks and saw no prospect of one until after the municipal elections. Perhaps, even then, Trinity men may have considered themselves lucky. It was not unusual in Oxford between the Wars to see undergraduates cycling through the City in their dressing gowns, towels around their necks, on their way from their lodgings to the College bathhouse – a steaming cellar where the young bloods sang 'Tickle up the Baby's Bottom' day after day, year after year, at the top of their unengaging voices.

But this was comparative modernity. Undergraduates in the later years of Queen Victoria (and until well after the First World War) usually took their baths in the evening, after tea, when the scouts had come on duty again. It was a hip bath standing up against a blazing fire, and the water, heated first in the scout's pantry at the foot of the stair, had to be brought up to eight or more sets (and then carried away). Patrick Gordon Walker, newly a Student (Fellow) of Christ Church in the 1920s, felt that dignity required a hip bath in his room. His scout and underscout (Fred Wheatley) could hardly say no. They brought up the water, but by stages it grew cooler and cooler (the wind setting in the east, the fire not drawing . . . the excuses grew weaker and weaker) until Gordon Walker's pride finally collapsed and he bathed with the rest. By this time hip baths in College rooms were no more than an occasional gesture to conservative dons, and undergraduates found their way to the College bathhouse. Yet scouts brought cans of hot water to bedrooms in the morning (and again just before dinner) until well after the Second World War.

Baths were followed by a drink before Hall, either with friends in one's room or, more often, all together in the Buttery. In the 1920s everybody in New College drank sherry in great quantity, although beer was preferred by Balliol. Dinner in Hall came next, for which, Dr Johnson said, a man must travel far before he finds anything better. Staircase scouts, in the nineteenth century, served their own men, at lightning speed. If

Preparing for Hall, Merton

"Dr Syntax entertained at the College" by Thomas Rowlandson

a man were 'sconced' for some solecism (like mentioning work, or a lady's name) it was his own scout who brought him a tankard of ale from the Buttery. Standards fell, alas, and personal service declined. Long after the Second World War a senior scout complained that the first glass of wine was poured out fifteen minutes before anyone sat down and all the vegs. were put straight on the table and not handed round, and this was at High Table too. . . 'I would never have dreamt of such a thing.' So much homely wisdom has gone. Who now remembers that sound and useful maxim: never drink claret in an east wind?

But the methodology had been as crude in the past, and the period of enlightenment brief. Both at High Table and down among the rabble the basic food for centuries, even up to the Second World War, was beef and mutton/lamb in great quantity dumped on the tables and hacked to pieces at will. Nathaniel Wedd, a Classics Fellow at King's who enjoyed shocking his colleagues, was heard to exclaim one evening, while he hacked at his joint, that his lamb was 'as hard to swallow as the Lamb of God'. If undergraduates wanted something better, they went out into the town. Michael Fane took ten friends to a private room at the Mitre, with its faded red wallpaper, glass cases of giant perch staring down from the walls and sporting prints of rod, gun and steeplechase. Fane's party was fed with stuffed ptarmigan and snipe, and served by two whiskered waiters 'in their garrulous subservience eloquent of Thackerayan scenes'.

Merton's food was always better than most and it remains so today. George Saintsbury described the efforts of the excellent Mr Betteris, chef in the 1860s; he was known for his hare soup and dressed crab, taken with half a (large) glass of some 'peculiarly excellent brown sherry'. In selecting Fellows it was said that at Merton the chief part of the examination was the High Table dinner to which candidates were invited and asparagus, cherry tart and other testing items always supplied. Thorold Rogers, the great economist, was once so dined (too well), and when the Fellows adjourned, hopped the length of their terrace overlooking the Meadow. When he had hopped his way back he was met by the dismissal 'you have hopped yourself out of your fellowship'; he caught the allusion (Herodotus VI 128–30) and had the wit and courage to reply: 'Hippocleides doesn't care'.

Undergraduates have always rushed through their meals. Fellows lingered: 'Edit, ergo est,' said Congreve of Gay. They also drank furiously. The Fellows of Lincoln and Brasenose, their Colleges back to back, used to entertain each other to a drunken dinner once a fortnight in Term: when over, they felt their way home along the interconnecting wall on Brasenose Lane. One day, in black darkness, a violent wind swept the crocodile across Radcliffe Square and the Fellows were found, at break of day, slowly following their leader (caps and gowns awry) round and round the Camera.

While some Scholar is reading grace
The Servants outside have a lark
That over, then brush into Hall
Their Masters to keep in the dark

Down at the tables are seated
Scores of Men with appetites sharp
The waiters all running about
And many with tongues there do carp

Wisken's name in Hall oft sounded
A message from some one is pop't
Meat tough, or something else wanting
Or knife in the gravy is drop't

Wisken, potatoes I do want
Wisken, do bring the greens this way
Wisken, ask if there's any soup
Wisken, do hear me what I say

In Oxford before the mid-century reforms, when scholarship was of less priority than it is (no doubt) today, Fellows preferred wine, women and horses to Dean Stanley's descriptions of the Holy Land. In the Common Room after dinner 'Alma Mater lay dissolved in port'. One entry in the betting book of the Senior Common Room of University College wagered that no mistake would be made in tasting blindfold twenty glasses of port, sherry, hock, claret and water.

Good vintage port at half a crown to three shillings and sixpence a bottle, long matured in College cellars, was most acceptable. Two Fellows (Lincoln and St John's) imported their wine directly from Oporto in 1824 and laid it down for twenty to thirty years in the College cellars; they then sold it to themselves at three shillings and four-pence a bottle. Port was drunk regularly until the last quarter of the nineteenth century; a few Fellows (the best) preferred claret, but white wine was ignored, and champagne

Even the lesser colleges drank well: Exeter's wine cellar, 1866

dismissed as 'a concoction intended to excite housemaids'. One critic has described pre-Reform Oxford as a 'quaint clerical club of convivial bachelors . . . over which the last rays of another sun of Hogarthian or Rowlandsonian revels had been cast – a world rarely disturbed by competitive examinations, serious religion, or real learning'. Life was too sheltered, too vinous. H. J. Bidden, a botanist in his cups, leapt into the quad with two hip baths, on one of which he sat while the other he placed on his head, challenging his fellow guests to open him up like an oyster. 'Beautiful city! So venerable, so lovely, so unravaged by the fierce intellectual life of our century' (Matthew Arnold, 1865).

Help (and Reform) was at hand. The general taste shifted to claret; teetotallers, almost unknown at an earlier date, left dinner prematurely and took pupils at eight. It was an early and unfortunate decision (soon discarded) when Froude and Newman persuaded the Fellows of Oriel to discontinue wine in the Common Room in favour of tea.

Muscular Christianity, Buchmanism and professionalism put an end to much real hard drinking, or nearly so, since F. E. Smith was left by his scout every night with a bottle of scotch and a cold supper laid out with champagne – in the morning it was all gone, all empty. A very nice man, said one scout of his Professor, but 'he do drink dreadful'. Yet *Blackwood's Magazine* was right to report, shortly before the First World War, that the consumption of wine in Colleges was trifling, far less than it had been fifty years earlier. Dr Johnson, while an undergraduate at Pembroke, claimed to have been a three bottle man (port) and none the worse for it. In the words of the 'Ode to the Bottle of Old Port':

How blest are the Tipplers whose head can outlive
The effects of four bottles of thee;
But the next dearest blessing that Heaven can give
Is to stagger home muzzy with three.

Naturally, undergraduates have never gone totally off their drink. Some Colleges brewed their own ale specifically to keep the young men out of the city alehouses. The Queen's College made an excellent beer that included an exceptionally fine variety called 'Chancellor', for special occasions.

A scout's day ended at or after 9 p.m. In days when dinner was served earlier, his duties had included taking supper to each undergraduate's rooms. He could be responsible for as many as half a dozen supper parties a night during Term, all at the same hour – a plate here, another there, a cork here, running from set to set. Supper in the eighteenth century was still an important affair, although Mr Edwards of Pembroke spoke of it disparagingly as 'a turnpike through which one must pass in order to get to bed'.

Suppers lost some of their importance when Hall dinner, the big meal of the day, was moved to the later, now standard, time of seven to seven thirty. But there was much demand for jollity and continuing entertainment throughout the rest of the evening; the scouts provided the ingredients, and it was they, next morning, who cleared the night's mess away. Scouts had their own specialities which they brewed in their pantries – negus (port or sherry, lemon and hot water, flavoured with spices), bishop (cinnamon, cloves, mace and all-spice, boiled port, the juice of half a lemon and grated nutmeg, sweetened to taste), beer flip (strong home-brewed beer with yolks of egg well beaten up, grated nutmeg, a little lemon, sugar and a piece of cinnamon), egg flip (the same with wine instead of beer) which was called 'Rum Booze' when strengthened (ill-advisedly) with half a pint of rum, sherry cobble (pounded ice and sugar, sherry, and strawberries drunk through a straw) and punches of all kinds, 'storatives', Brown Betty, claret cup, slig, and a collection of Oxford night-caps. 'After supper', wrote an undergraduate to his father, 'we had egg-flip, punch, cordial, and bishop, about a gallon to each of us. . . .'

It was all very jolly and unlicensed, even if girls were wholly absent. What actually took place was 'old, amiable ragging and rotting . . . parlour rowdiness with cushions and sofas' among the Good Eggs of St Mary's. Manly young throats swallowed fiery alcohol and expelled hearty noise, singing 'Up in a Balloon, Boys' and 'Have you seen the Shah', drinking toasts to a chorus 'Once so merrily hopped she – twice so merrily hopped she – thrice so merrily hopped she – sing hi, sing ho, sing he' when at each 'hopped she' every Good Egg took a sip from his glass and emptied it at the last chorus. Then also there was communal singing (between the Wars) in Ruskin College, hearty, wholesome stuff, fervent voice, free fellowship, 'Annie Laurie', 'Tom Brown's Body' and the rest, when even Dataller found that the 'hefty, hearty son of toil' gave him a pain.

From COLLEGE LIFE

Narcotics disagree with some people?

Undergraduate 'wines', after Hall, were in practice punch parties with a little food (cold duck perhaps, or something of the kind), but they were not orgies; the supper that followed was less controlled. Young Mark Pattison's first 'wine' was a disaster –'oh, the icy coldness, the dreary Egyptian blankness of that "wine" ', when the guests slipped away and Pattison was left alone with an almost untouched dessert. Others, under more confident and attractive hosts, were far more successful. J. F. Nixon, Dean of College at King's, held glee meetings once a week after Hall, at which he sang Victorian catches and they, madrigals for male voices; in the interval hot buttered buns were handed

Vincent's Club at dinner, c 1900. "Too definitely Dark Blue and Leander Pink, but the best…"

Drawn & Engraved by R. Cruikshank.

Published May 1.1824 by Sherwood, Jones & Co.

Flooring of Mercury: or Burning the Oaks, a Scene in Tom Quadrangle.

From THE ENGLISH SPY

round, anchovy toast, Borneo cigars and Tintara wine. Then there were the smoking concerts ('smokers') of that great decade before August 1914, when the young creatures 'did nigger business' and startled their seniors with risqué stories and light comedy songs ('she was fat; she was fat; she was awful fat. She weighed at least twenty stone in nothing but her hat'). All Colleges, both in Oxford and Cambridge, had 'smokers', where traditional songs were sung in dense clouds of tobacco smoke, and undergraduates stamped their boots on the old oak dining tables.

Every function in each busy Term was served by College scouts, and this was true too of the many Oxford clubs. The most élitist, The Club, consisted (in Spooner's day) of seven Heads of Houses and five other members, and it dined together every other week during Term; another, almost equally select, was 'The Tutors' Club'. Cambridge had 'The Family', a club of Heads of Houses, university officers, professors and dons; it was distinguished by such novel foods as buffalo hump and capercailye and its members played whist into the early hours of the morning. Cambridge's Chit-Chat Club, for both senior and junior members of King's and Trinity, met every Saturday evening for discussion of papers, serious and light, accompanied by the usual claret cup, hot buns and anchovy toast. Young heads could not always hold it. At a Carbonari dinner of 1907 that included Rupert Brooke and Hugh Dalton ('atheist exquisites and anarchist Bedlamists'), Gerald Shrove proposed the toast: 'The King, God damn him!' The gyps were scandalised, the news spread through the town, and the Chetwynd society, a social club for brawn rather than brain, threw Dalton into the Fountain. It was the old battle between 'highbrows' and 'hearties'.

A bewildering variety of subcultures formed all over the Universities and within Colleges themselves. One of the peculiar charms of Oxford, to Goronwy Rees, was that one might stumble across such minicultures in the most unlikely corners. There was the Canning Club, a Tory group that spent its time (before Curzon became its Secretary) drinking mulled claret, playing whist and taking sweepstakes on the Derby. Others were the Raleigh, Durham and Chatham Clubs (also political), the Williams and Hardwicke (for lawyers), a multitude of essay clubs, Balliol's Brackenbury Society (open to scholars) and Devorguilla (to athletes and 'fashionables'). Ralph Marret, an austere and largely unlovable character who ended as Rector of Exeter and Vice-Chancellor, calculated that as an undergraduate he had belonged to about eighteen of these societies, although half were the 'abortive creation of some master-mind, and lasted only a term or two'.

In reformed Oxford, undergraduates were no longer allowed to enter pubs, and pubs remained forbidden until after the Second World War. Smart dining clubs replaced taverns and hotels: Vincent's was the best but 'too definitely Dark Blue and Leander Pink', or the Grid, which Michael Fane preferred as displaying the most completely normal undergraduate existence and a willingness to elect – rather than co-opt – its members (although naturally from only seven or eight Colleges . . .); Vincent's was the 'last stronghold of muscular supremacy'. OUDS (the Oxford University Dramatic Society) had its own room in George Street until the Second World War – large, ugly and modern over a big cheap shop opposite the New Theatre, with pictures of actors on the walls – 'a proclamation of mountebank worship'. The Bullingdon, with its grey beaver hats, velvet coats and white trousers striped with vivid blue was a delightful anachronism even before 1914. The Union was too undiscriminating: 'Manchester and Birmingham could have produced a result very similar'. Colleges had their own dining clubs – even little Hertford, where the undergraduates 'dined glorious in white waist-coats with cerise revers – the Hertford colours'.

Clubs were well patronised. Sir John Masterman, as a young don at Christ Church in the early 1920s, continued his undergraduate habit of lunching two or three times a week at Vincent's during Term, with the occasional dinner or tea to boot; Vincent's had its own permanent Steward and club rooms in the High, and one of its best features, Masterman found, was a house dinner consisting of soup, fish, joint, two sweets, savoury and cheese, all at half a crown a head, with beer, tea and coffee thrown in, and letters stamped free of charge; Vincent's was a bargain even for the day. Others were much more expensive. But somehow the undergraduates paid, as somehow nowadays they pay when they are charged £50 each time they deposit a colleague in Mercury (the fine was once £5), 80 guineas rather than five for a double ticket to a Commemoration Ball, and £60 per head for dinner with the Bullingdon Club (Bollinger, smoked salmon wrapped around caviare, turbot in champagne sauce, wild duck in Armagnac).

After all, there is *something* to be said for this. Oxford societies and clubs kept young men out of mischief and brought emolument (and genuine pleasure, too) to generations of scouts. Very little could have existed without College servants, and when scouts departed a large share of social Oxford went with them. Tom Brown, writing home on his first term, told Geordie (his pal) that in the Oxford of his day the scout was an institution. And so he was.

BULLINGDON

THE STATUE OF MERCURY

"Bruce", groom and horsedealer to the incautious undergraduates of Merton. An entry in the college register for 1882 recommends "that the servants be warned by the Junior Bursar that any of them found speaking to Bruce will be liable to dismissal"...

Chapter 6

A SCOUT'S LIFE (1)

Ultimately, scouts found themselves modernised out of existence. But some compensation was to be found in the disappearance simultaneously of so many of the worst manifestations of servility and dependence. 'It is an ill worm that has no turning', as Vanessa Bell is supposed to have said, a mis-use of wise saws that sister Viginia 'improved' when she invented 'taking the bull by the udders', and 'a stitch in nine saves time'.

The threat of 'loss of character' and arbitrary dismissal was probably the most unenviable in a domestic servant's experience, although here at least the College scout, within a very broad range of competence and performance, had security of tenure and a place for life. You seldom heard, said the Butler of the Principal of Brasenose, of servants leaving a College until they were pensioned off. Albert Thomas was sure that the reason for secure employment lay not in the work, which was much the same for servants everywhere, but in three separate characteristics of College employment, the first that College servants slept out in their own homes, a second that they were considered as more than just domestic servants and thus nobodies, but third, because they worked under men alone, and it was *women employers* who were the cause of so much unrest.

All the same, there was class prejudice of every kind in and out of College. A butler, writing about men servants in *Nineteenth Century* (June 1892), spoke of the 'refined cruelty that is perpetrated upon servants by employers and their families', the amount of which could not be described; 'let better service be required,' he said, 'but let the

"Old Symmonds" and "Porter and Green". College servants from Corpus, c 1870

servant be treated as a man.' College servants were never in the cruel, forlorn position of the solitary 'general', usually in a lower-middle/upper-working class family, or of the 'slavey' in a bed-and-breakfast house, overworked, isolated and vulnerable.

Until well after the industrialisation of Oxford in the 1920s, when Morris Motors at Cowley became the benchmark for local wages, employment as a College scout was much sought-after. Scout families became dynasties, and replacements or new positions were allocated by patronage or inheritance. College servants came from 'good artisan families', from the same type that supplied printers for Oxford's Clarendon Press; 'one got into Colleges by recommendation – it went in families quite a lot'; 'people were very glad to get their boys in as "boys" to a servant on a staircase'. College

The servants of a small college, Pembroke, 1890

domestic servants were 'rather a class to themselves, they were greatly respected; it was a distinction until well into the inter-war period' (Miss C. V. Butler). John Burnett is surely right when he argues that the falling status of domestic service was a Victorian phenomenon and that in any case the position of servants in large establishments (he was talking of noblemen's houses although the same was true of Colleges) was far higher than in small; domestic work was 'chiefly resented in proportion to its degree of social isolation and anonymity' (*Useful Toil*, 1974).

It is difficult to obtain any satisfactory scale for the value of money; £1 sterling in 1850 could buy £20 today. Nowadays, servants at Colleges are earning, by the hour, much what they earned by the week as recently as the 1920s. This means little on its own. The stipend of College Fellows themselves in the 1870s/1880s was usually about £300 p.a.; many did not teach, although a teaching Fellow who received fees directly from individual undergraduates should have been able to make up his income to £500/£600. In Cambridge, where 'coaching' seems to have been better organised, a really first-class coach could accumulate £700/£800, which amounted at the time to a respectable, upper-middle-class income.

In practice, however, few of the new generation of married Fellows from the 1870s had an income of more than £500 a year, and nobody under the rank of Head of House, other than a few privileged Professors, earned as much as £1000. Yet their wives all gave dinner parties, said Mrs Humphrey Ward, furnished their homes in North Oxford 'with Morris papers, old chests and cabinets and blue pots', and went to their dinners in Liberty gowns. It was said that middle-class families in Oxford, with two children and two maids, could live comfortably and make short visits to the seaside, even if they were in no position as yet to afford journeys on the Continent.

Times were harder from the 1880s when the agricultural depression reduced rents, College revenues, and therefore Fellows' stipends. Oscar Browning, whose Fellowship had been worth £300 when he came into residence in King's in 1876, found himself with less than half that amount a decade later.

Alternative employment: Morris Motors, Cowley, 1920s

It is possible, then, to form a more realistic idea of what a scout's wage was worth, and the conclusion must be that before Oxford expectations were raised by Morris Motors, College scouts were relatively well off. Certainly this was the case by comparison with agricultural workers nearby, where Oxfordshire before the Great War was well known to be one of the worst-paid agricultural counties in England. Early in the last century a handbook gave the following guide lines for the wages of *resident* male domestic servants, and these rates seem to have remained pretty standard up to the First World War:

Butler	£50 p.a.
Footman	£24 p.a.
Coachman	£28 p.a.
Under-footman	£20 p.a.

An Oxford scout was paid about £40 p.a. before the First World War, on top of which he could expect his tips and 'perquisites'. On the other hand, he was non-resident and entitled to neither board nor lodging.

By the 1920s a scout's relative position had in some senses deteriorated. Fred Wheatley, as a scout's boy at Christ Church in 1926, was paid 14 shillings a week, when he could have earned £2 or more on the assembly line at Cowley. But then Morris Motors, in those days, gave absolutely no security, made its workers redundant when the orders ran out, worked them hard for six months and then put them on half time or no time at all for the rest of the year. . . . Colleges were more secure, and since by now they gave a twelve-month basic rate, 'you probably caught them up in the factories because they would lose so many weeks, and you *knew* you couldn't lose a week . . . you had a sense of fairly comfortable livelihood' (B. W. Standen).

In those days before Beveridge, security above all was prized. Most Colleges by the 1920s had organised a contributory pension scheme for their domestic staff. It may have brought only £50 p.a. at the age of 60, but it was better than in domestic service generally where 'perhaps one in a hundred butlers gets a sort of pension enough to keep him out of a work house'. It was the kind of security enjoyed only by central and local government employees, by members of the armed services, by railway servants, and by the police.

As for the College wage itself, a staircase scout in the 1920s earned between thirty shillings and two pounds a week, about double the rate pre-war. If taken together with security and the addition, sometimes considerable, of tips and 'emoluments', it compared not unfavourably with a weekly wage of about 45 shillings for labourers in the Engineering and Allied trades. By the mid-1930s, when the security of College employment must indeed have been a prize, wages for College scouts had risen to between

Billy Garrett, Trinity Porter

The servants of Hertford, 1912

£2.10s. and £3, a 'very good' wage indeed, on which Percy Abbs, at least, felt himself able to marry. It was after the Second World War that the wages of scouts dropped behind, and even then there were men in Oxford who preferred the quiet life and companionship of College service to the hurly-burly of motor manufacturing at Cowley.

It was not the basic wage that mattered; there were other ways of making a living. Shoe cleaning, for example, was paid for separately, and there was a fee for taking clothes to the cleaner. Even in the 1920s scouts were paid for anything in excess of usual duties. 'Bearing a cut' was the conventional term at Christ Church for the half-crown fee due to the scout from undergraduates who were sick, caught short, or unable to reach the lavatory in time after an over-abundant debauch. One scout even had his own special card printed:

To

Bear you a Cut 2/6

Fred Wheatley, who had married young and now found himself supporting a family, raised his weekly earnings in the mid 1930s as a staircase scout at Queen's to an average of £9; he was able to pick up a great deal by serving at all kinds of parties in his spare time which he would then supplement by much window cleaning for the College – the kind of occupation, traditional to College servants, that came increasingly to be handled by outside contractors.

Before the *First* World War, there was always work, out of hours, servicing the endless frivolities of *la Grande Époque:*

There are dances, flirtations at Nuneham,
Flower-shows, the processions of Eights;
There's a list stretching usque ad Lunam
Of concerts, and lunches, and fêtes. . . .

(A. T. Quiller Couch, 1893)

The University College barge at Eights' Week, c 1905: profitable employment dispensing teas

Eights' week was busiest for the 'overheated scout', whose (profitable) duty it was to dispense teas on the College barge and supply the 'changeless' lunches of cold chicken and salmon mayonnaise. Political, debating, literary and social clubs and societies required service, and every year Colleges had their Gaudés (the 'correct' version of the more familiar Gaudy – a College dinner for past members). Then, money was to be earned in serving teas at the Union, or managing (with wife) College digs in Merton Street and Magpie Lane, Beaumont Street, St John's Street, Walton Street and Museum Road.

Vacation Conferences are a creature of the present, although they had begun with Oxford Group functions in the 1930s. Scouts and their 'boys' were previously 'released' by the Colleges during the Long Vacation and found their living at holiday hotels in the Highlands, the Lake District, Newquay and the West Country. Basic wages could be as low as 25 shillings a week, plus keep, but tips were retained and if one were lucky enough to be 'on the lounges' for the evening, with tips of twopence or threepence on the drink, £1 could be earned by the end of the day – equivalent, after all, to a week's wage.

Earnings before the Second World War were not, then, the real problem; there were others. The suspicion of master/mistress for servants has always been the curse of domestic service. A servant's job is to work intimately with private possessions, and it can be done properly only with trust. *Peter Priggins: The College Scout* (1840) is obsessed with 'pillage' – *omnibus hic vitium lecti factoribus* ('this vice common to all bedmakers', a donnish derivation that readers will instantly recognise as from Horace's *Satires* 1:3:1 where Horace refers to the vice of all prima donnas: tiresomely unending song). *Verdant Green*, another book of this genre, is quite as bad. And 'how in the world are youngsters with unlimited credit, plenty of ready money and fast tastes, to be kept from making fools and blackguards of themselves up here?' thought Sanders (*Tom Brown at Oxford*); there was something in what he said. Scouts were older, experienced men, and they knew how to handle their young charges:

Vacation work in Brighton for Pembroke scouts in the 1930s

A University Extension course in Balliol, summer 1887. Benjamin Jowett sleeps in the front row . . .

Balliol shows its political colours: delegates to the Labour Party Conference, July 1908

La, Sir, a gent like you wouldn't give a breakfast without a shoulder-of-lamb and a turkey. You must have cider-cup and beer-cup at your lunch. It will never do to have ten gentlemen to wine, and only three dishes of dessert, for a gent like you, Sir. . . .

(R. Thomson, *Almae Matres* 1857)

Wallace Blair called the scout of his freshman hero a 'hoary villain of incredible experience [and] cynical obsequiousness'. The young freshman of eighteen who came up from one of Britain's great public schools, said Leslie Stephen, showed a 'negation of all useful knowledge which is, in its way, a really impressive phenomenon'; they were easy victims, and often misled.

College Comforts. A Freshman taking possession of his Rooms.

From THE ENGLISH SPY

Freshman and his parents — beginning residence: arrival of "absolute necessities". Engraving from The Graphic, *1880's*

It is true that the system lent itself to exploitation. The Colleges, merely echoing a practice common among hoteliers and caterers even today, paid low wages that anticipated comfortable supplements from 'perks'. In the nineteenth century and before, Colleges supplied their undergraduates with nothing other than the rooms themselves; when a freshman arrived he was expected to pay 'Thirds' – i.e. two thirds of the cost of the previous occupant's furniture, receiving himself two thirds from his own successor. It was an arrangement that gave rise to handsome commissions for the unscrupulous, so that by the last decades of Victorianism it was generally forbidden by the College authorities. Meanwhile, much opportunity existed for deception, and freshmen were warned to choose their rooms by the reputation of the scout rather than the quality of the furnishings. The first days were by far the worst:

In the sad and sodden street
To and fro
Flit the fever-stricken feet
Of the freshers as they meet,
Come and go
Ever buying, buying, buying,
When the shopmen stand supplying,
Vying, vying
All they know,
While the Autumn lies a-dying
Sad and low.

(Frowde, *Echoes from the Oxford Magazine, 1890*)

The principal calamity of the freshman, said George Colman the Younger in 1830, arose from his ignorance of 'oeconomicks'. The best scouts felt it to be their responsibility to advise their young men on the shops they should use if they were to avoid being 'stung' – 'you were a scout to them, you became their friend'. . . . Unfortunately, others entered into alliance with local tradesmen on commission, or

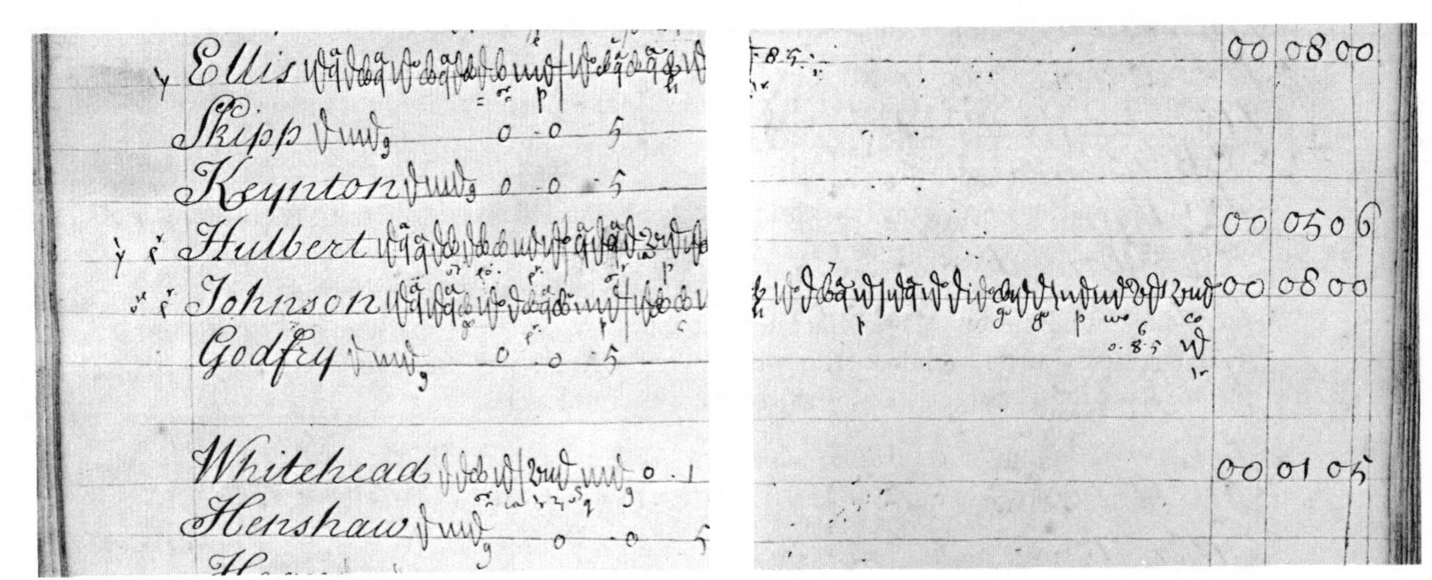

Dr. Johnson's weekly battels ... in code

bought and sold property for themselves. Oxford, in those days, lived almost entirely off the University, and many shops closed altogether during the vacation. Wine, tea, sugar, coals, candles, bed and table linens were brought to George Colman (*Random Records*, 1830) by his Christ Church scout and bedmaker, both helped by their spouses; these auxiliaries demanded 'no further emolument than that which arises from their being the conjugal helpmates of the stipendiary despoilers'. Augustus Hare's first day in College was a levée – 'coalman's fee, if you please, sir – half a crown', the buttery boy next, the scout, a man who declared himself the sole agent of an important magazine, and a vendor of flannels and 'dressing robes'. Gentlemen, said Daniel Defoe, took larger quantities of provisions so that their custom was more valuable; tradesmen thought that to obtain it 'a Gratuity to the Servant was not ill bestow'd'.

'Commissions' leave a nasty taste in the mouth of those who pay them, but what really hurt were 'perquisites'. Oxford scouts (like Cambridge gyps) worked to a recognised scale that, to their credit, they seldom abused – a small commission on coals, candles or matches from their own scullery stores. A College scout, writing in *Belgravia* (June 1873), was right to say that any master of the 'most ordinary liberality' would never blame a servant for taking his 'fair, customary and recognised perquisites'.

Unfortunately, few masters could overcome the suspicion that all was not perfectly well: 'Honesty and respectability, indeed! – and in a scout?' Ignorance of each other and mutual misunderstanding – it was the kind of social block that in its most extreme forms brought trusted servants with knives to their mistresses' throats at the outbreak of the Indian Mutiny, and then blew them from the mouths of British cannon at the end.

"Perquisites of a butler". A sketch commemorating the curtailment of butlery expenses at Christ Church in 1866

Meanwhile, all worked smoothly so long as neither side knew enough of the other and both obeyed the rules. It was 'a perpetual kind of dishonesty, you know', said one Bursar of All Souls (Sir E. L. Woodward); 'they wouldn't steal money at all, but they'd steal cigarettes and help themselves to drinks . . . this had always gone on, and it was a thing you always expected them to do . . . it was just rather like the army, a perpetual, very mild, pinching.'

The scouts were not to blame when the Bursar of Queen's developed the theory that vintage port, once uncorked, lasted only three quarters of an hour before it became common tawny: the bottles were whisked off the table once the sacred moment had passed and drunk with appreciation in the pantry. Drunkenness, unfortunately, became something of an occupational disease among scouts. Woodward's scout in Corpus, earlier this century, was 'very old and about to retire; and he got slightly drunk every night'; the legend at Corpus – not wholly right, perhaps, but not entirely wrong – was that the scouts did not go home as they were supposed to do at 11.00 a.m. but that they sat on in the scouts' room just behind the Kitchen and drank beer solidly until they came on duty again at lunch time. The besetting temptation of College servants, said one preacher, was 'immoderate indulgence in drink' which 'the cultivation of home affections, the chaste love of wife and the fond endearments of children' could alone resolve.

Scouts, in any case, were not really in a position where their 'perquisites' *could* become extravagantly large. Chefs did much better and 'Coquus', the head cook at 'with an official salary higher than that of a resident Tutor and perquisites reckoned to be worth another couple of hundred at least'.

Far more acceptable than perquisites, although troublesome even then, were legitimate tips, and these could be large indeed. Even early in the eighteenth century it could cost a guinea to get away from a dinner party. As Dean Swift wrote to Stella in 1710: 'Lord Halifax is always teasing me to go to his country house, which will cost me a guinea to his servants and 12s coach hire, and he shall be hanged first.' A country-house

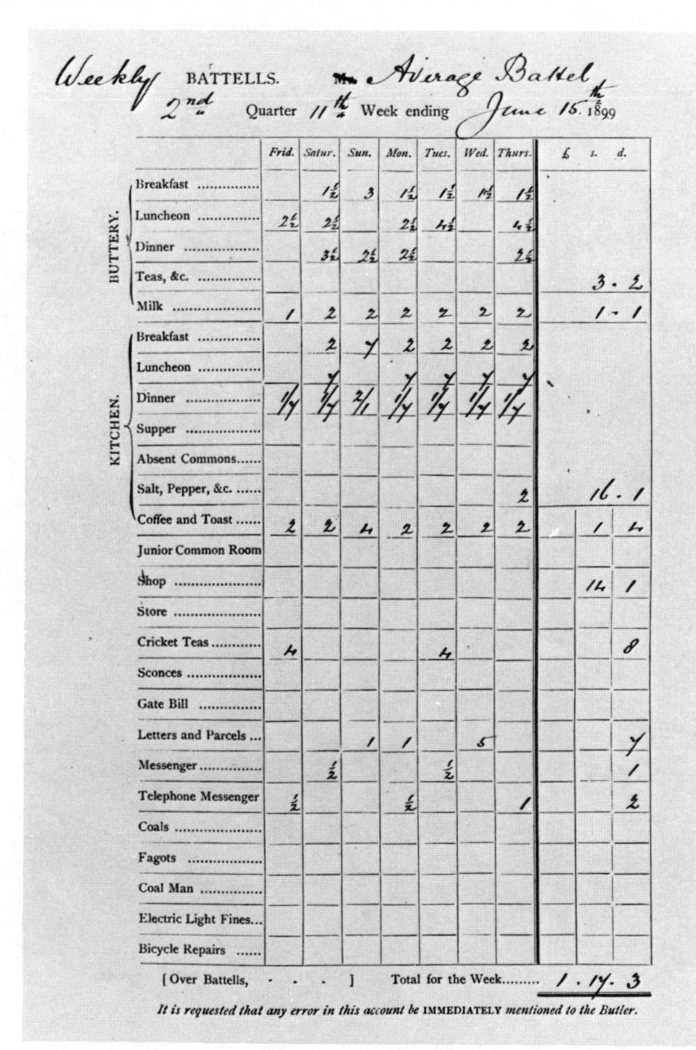

Weekly BATTELLS. ~~Mr.~~ Average Battel
2nd Quarter 11th Week ending June 15th 1899

		Frid.	Satur.	Sun.	Mon.	Tues.	Wed.	Thurs.	£	s.	d.
BUTTERY.	Breakfast		1½	3	1½	1½	1½	1½			
	Luncheon	2½	2½		2½	4½		4½			
	Dinner		3½	2½	2½			2½			
	Teas, &c.									3	2
	Milk	1	2	2	2	2	2	2		1	1
KITCHEN.	Breakfast		2	7	2	2	2	2			
	Luncheon										
	Dinner	1/7	1/7	2/1	1/7	1/7	1/7	1/7			
	Supper										
	Absent Commons										
	Salt, Pepper, &c.							2		16	1
	Coffee and Toast	2	2	4	2	2	2	2		1	4
	Junior Common Room										
	Shop									14	1
	Store										
	Cricket Teas	4				4					8
	Sconces										
	Gate Bill										
	Letters and Parcels			1	1		5				7
	Messenger		½			½					1
	Telephone Messenger	½			½			1			2
	Coals										
	Fagots										
	Coal Man										
	Electric Light Fines										
	Bicycle Repairs										

[Over Battells, . . .] Total for the Week......... 1 . 17 . 3

It is requested that any error in this account be IMMEDIATELY *mentioned to the Butler.*

From a Balliol prospectus, 1900. "A bill like this is sent to each student every week; usually all the bills of a term are paid together at the beginning of the next term"

Part of an undergraduate's expenses

guest in Edwardian England was still paying out in tips on a scale every bit as high as eighteenth-century 'vails' – a sovereign to the butler, half a sovereign upwards for the chauffeur, five shillings to the lady's maid, perhaps as much as five pounds altogether for a ten-day shooting party. Tips were univeral and well understood. Each Victorian household distributed from a shilling to half a crown on Boxing Day to chimney-sweeps, beadles, lamplighters, watermen, dustmen, street cleaners, newspaper boys, general postmen, two-penny postmen and waits.

It was all part of the progress towards a proper national wage, and as wages became more proportionate to needs both perquisites and tips declined; eighteenth-century corruption in Justice, in the Customs and Excise, became Victorian probity on £1,000 a year. Scouts did not always allow for this when they complained at those undergraduates who had given ten shillings a term as the standard tip in 1900, and then gave ten shillings still for years and years into the 1960s. But when College wages were low, the proportion of total income accounted for by tips could be substantial. One staircase of eight 'sets' at Christ Church (where the rate of tipping was admittedly twice or more that to be expected in poorer Colleges) brought at least £16 each term to the staircase scout in the 1920s and £8 to the scout's boy; it was known to have risen much higher, up to 40 to 50 per cent added by tips to the basic wage.

Queen's in 1937 abolished all tipping; the burden had become too embarrassing for the poorer undergraduates and it was felt better to raise the level of College wages. Good though the idea was – the Dean was Oliver Franks – and popular with many of the scouts themselves, it was not adopted by other Colleges until after the Second World War.

Gratuities, then, were a solid part of the scout's wage. They were better for both giver and receiver when paid in cash than in kind. The practice of signing beer-orders (a kind of cheque payable in ale at the College buttery) was not to be recommended. The boot-black, for example, got a beer-order from every man in college. When John Venn, as an undergraduate in nineteenth-century Cambridge, asked his College bootblack how he ever managed to get through it all, the reply was, 'We works it off, Sir, we works it off.' Then there were so many others to be tipped at the end of term – scouts, messengers, underporters and a string of boatmen.

The subtleties and refinements of tipping needed all the experience of a seasoned passenger on an old Cunarder. Servants themselves, although fully aware that gratuities formed a legitimate part of their earnings, never welcomed them. Bob Gammon, not long ago, was asked whether he preferred tips or a higher basic wage; his reply, naturally, was that he preferred the basic wage, 'provided it was the right one.'

Chapter 7

A SCOUT'S LIFE (2)

Oxford Colleges between the Wars were small and still intimate. Dons were mostly resident bachelors and domestic labour was plentiful and cheap. From the 1940s Colleges were required to take far greater numbers both of undergraduates and of dons, and such greater numbers demanded closer control. Professional managers from the hotel and catering trades were as yet a thing of the future, and the great and rapid expansion of the conference business was still far away. All the same, a different technique was necessary, and the job of the College's domestic management could no longer be entrusted to burnt-out and redundant dons.

One of the trials of a scout's life, for which salvation came normally from a healthy and vigorous sense of humour, was the preaching of well-meaning but insensitive dons. What with the Tractarianism of Newman's earlier days (very Holy and very High Church), *der Puseyismus* in the mid-century, then Keble, the C. of E. and 'holy joy' at Cuddesdon, scouts were subjected, within a single century, to generations of preachers and much earnest, missionary endeavour. Jack, turning serious, told his pal Tom Brown something he had never said before: there was too much 'Common-room Christianity' in Oxford, 'belief in a dead God', and it would be 'sore work, work for our strongest and wisest shipping off the comfortable wine-party religion in which we are all wrapped up. . . .' These were desperate days indeed. One evening an undergraduate marched up to High Table at King's and presented a scroll to the Provost 'in the Name of Jesus Christ, Our Lord'. The awkward hush, before the man was led out by the Tutor, was broken only by the voice of Oscar Browning: 'Would you mind passing the potatoes.'

Cranham Street in Jericho, the north Oxford home of the upper working classes: scouts, printers and railwaymen

Not everything in Chapel was heavy going, although it is an uncomfortable thought that the first, cast-iron stove was installed at Lincoln only in 1838. Dr Blackiston (President of Trinity), finding himself in some difficulty with his own ornate handwriting by candlelight, warned his congregation that some of them were 'frivolous, of course'; he glanced at his script and repeated it; he glanced again – 'I beg your pardon; some of you are followers of Christ.'

The standard was uneven. A Tutor of Christ Church said of certain doctors of divinity that their scarlet robes concealed less learning than might be supposed; and in a University so wedded to the classics whatever learning there was might turn out to be the wrong kind – 'In the sermon I have just preached', said the Reverend William Spooner, 'whenever I said Aristotle, I meant St Paul.' But 'the Spoo' was known for his difficulties. Preaching on the topic of sin and its blandishments he found himself confronting the peril of being misled: 'Do not be mizzled,' he warned, straining to read his text. 'No, not mizzled, mished. Well, mizzled *or* mished.'

Both for dons and undergraduates alike, College life required attendance at Chapel right up to the First World War, and it was only the war veterans of 1919 who finally ignored it. College servants were expected themselves to be Church-goers, although they were seldom admitted freely to the ordinary range of chapel services.

The Rev. H. E. Clayton, Fellows' Chaplain at Magdalen, was something of specialist in evangelising among College servants. He was sure himself that servants had no wish for special services in College chapels; 'they do not like being treated as a class, they prefer their parish churches'. If Colleges were to provide their own services (as two Colleges actually did when he spoke in 1892) the preaching, he advised, should be simple and not too formal, there should be 'hearty singing', and a time would have to be chosen that would not interfere with the performance of domestic duties.

Not long before, the Rev. William Ince, then Sub-Rector of Exeter, made great efforts to serve the religious needs of the College staff. During the rebuilding of the College Chapel from seventeenth-century block to George Gilbert Scott's more fashionable and commodious scale model of the Sainte Chappelle, Ince held regular services for the College and its servants at St Michael's along the Broad. Once the new Chapel was built, he took an active part in conducting a second evening service every Sunday during Term for the special benefit of College servants, their families and friends; it was done with the aid of a voluntary choir of undergraduates and it became, the good man often thought, 'the brightest and liveliest and most inspiriting of all the Services of the day performed in Chapel'. At the servants' evening service on Advent Sunday, 1863, Ince found occasion to commend the example of the recently deceased steward, Thomas Hewlett, thirty five years with the College, starting from 'the very lowest situation'. Hewlett's diligence, integrity and skill had earned him the respect of both superior and inferiors: 'See'st thou a man delight in his business? He shall stand before Kings, he shall not stand before men.' This faithful servant had been followed to the grave by every Fellow of the College who could possibly attend, and 'here surely is an encouragement for you the younger men and boys'.

Colleges followed their separate ways. Some admitted servants to their ordinary services, and Albert Annets, a servant at Oriel for a large part of the nineteenth century, was known for missing not a single service in Chapel. But Alec Lyne, just over the road at Corpus, when asked whether scouts had open access to Chapel in his own College between the Wars, replied: 'Oh no, that was a bit out of bounds, yes, I rather think so.' Most Colleges simply made arrangements for their servants to be free at an appropriate hour on Sunday mornings so that they could attend a place of public worship elsewhere, and this, nearer home and in the company of their families, was no doubt what they themselves preferred.

Some responsibility, often lightly felt, might be attached among clerical dons to the religious welfare of their servants, although the effect may simply have been to ensure that scouts spent on religious observance what time they had left from the day of rest. Among the scouts themselves, attitudes varied very widely about the place that Colleges might take in their social life. Some, quite legitimately, felt themselves to be

Magdalen college servants in the 1930s

Servants' Eleven, Balliol, 1902

Scouts off duty in the 1930s. The Oxford Servants' Eight in Cambridge for their annual race (top left). The Brasenose fire brigade: most colleges had private fire brigades before the Second World War (bottom left). Marriage under the oars (right)

doing a job, adequately if not outstandingly well, in return for a sufficient security and a reasonable wage. It did not follow that they received, or expected, any more. David Pomeroy (a scout at Corpus) was once asked what scouts did together out of College:

> *Nothing. In some cases, there's one or two that possibly goes fishing with each other, but apart from that they're purely friends when they're in College, and when we go home, we go home, and leave our work behind us, you know. That just about wraps it up.*

Inevitably, unsocial hours shut scouts off from so many others, and this, together with the difficulty of seeing wives and children, was one of the great drawbacks of the job. It was not always so, since there were scouts who found sufficient social contact within their own community playing cards, darts and shove ha'penny in the Scouts' Room, or drinking in the College's favourite pub with other scouts, with undergraduates and with the occasional affable and condescending don.

When scouts were in their hey-day, in and before the inter-War years, a kind of community of College servants existed in Oxford. They had their own club in the Iffley Road which ran dances in the Masonic Hall two or three times a year and kept a pavilion for bowls and tennis. Most Colleges had Christmas parties for their servants, with a sit-down meal, party games, whist and dancing to records. A separate party was organised for children, 'if anything the better of the two', with its Christmas tree, conjurer, clown and perhaps a film. Servants' outings – charabancs to the sea, trips down to a show in London, picnics in the Cotswolds – seem to have died out in the 1950s, but they had once been common and very popular.

Scouts were keen on sport and some were themselves considerable sportsmen on the river in 'fours' and even to the standard of county cricket. Scouts ran their own United Colleges Servants' Cricket Club, and in 1950 the Oxford University and College Servants' Rowing Club was still in existence and celebrating its centenary;

A Christmas party in Trinity in the 1930s

simultaneously, servants' tennis, bowls and rowing clubs were competing biennially with Cambridge. Before the War a four-day regatta was organised by and for College servants during the Long Vacation, followed by bump suppers, and as recently as 1950 the report of the Servants' Rowing Club recorded the busiest season ever. No conferences interrupted the calm of the summer vacation, and scouts played cricket together three of four afternoons a week, all dressed in white flannels, sweaters and cricket caps 'just the same as the others did'.

Now scouts are nearly gone, conferences fill Colleges out of Term, 'part-time women' substitute. College servants wear white coats when they once wore suits and bowler hats; some even sport caterers' blue. Young gentlemen once dressed for dinner and the scouts at High Table received a clothing allowance for the dress clothes they wore every night: collar and stiff shirt, bow tie and tail coat. Now, undergraduates dress anyhow, 'and all this long hair right down to their shoulders,' said one old scout, 'I hate to see it'.

Chapter 8

FELLOWS AND THEIR SCOUTS

Scouts, in their attitude to dons, have shown exaggerated, perhaps even unmerited, respect. The Fellows were their employers and, as Dr Johnson said, subordination 'tends greatly to human happiness'. When Jonathan Swift, in his 'humorous advice to servants', urged that in quarrelling together the servant class should remember its common enemy 'which is your master and lady', he was thinking of ordinary domestics (in Anglo-Ireland, too) and not of the cushioned life of the College scout, free of womanly competition and comfortably in alliance with resident Fellows against fleeting undergraduates.

An immense gulf existed between levels of educational attainment at all points in the social pyramid. It was so vast that the gardener at Tolworth, astonished by the Master of Pembroke's knowledge of pears, cried out that God was Great. Servants were in no position to challenge a don like Oscar Browning whom a social equal, E. F. Benson, described as a 'genius flawed by abysmal fatuity'; Browning it was who, on his return from London one day, quite casually let fall that William II was one of the nicest emperors *he* had ever met.

These scholars published little, a failing that was 'supposed to be characteristic of gifted dons', and they left no trace. Yet in Oxford and Cambridge, and within their own Colleges, there was 'nothing so imperious as a Fellow upon his dunghill, nothing so contemptible abroad'. It was said of one scientist, indeed, that he found some difficulty in remembering that he was only the editor of *Nature* and not its author.

Although College Fellows had been permitted to marry from the latter part of the

The grand "sitter" of a senior don at Christ Church before the First World War

"The old order changeth yielding place to the new"

nineteenth century, a high proportion, even between the Wars, still lived as bachelors in College. Corpus scouts complained that 'they look upon us and say, six days shalt thou labour, but on the Sabbath thou shalt do a damn sight more'. In the 1890s they spent their Christmas vacation hob-nobbing with the nobility, where a Howard child classified his family's guests either as 'dukes' (who shot) or 'philosophers' (who did not).

Then, during the Easter holidays, Fellows left Oxford to take advantage of the sunny, cool weather now to be found in Italy, Greece and the Riviera. In summer they went to Cornwall, Wales and Scotland, although those of hardier temperament and independent means were off to Baden-Baden, Wiesbaden, Rome, Vienna and Constantinople. The last month before the new academic year was passed agreeably in a London club. Indeed Fellowships, in those days, were 'devilish snug things . . . for the indigent middle classes'.

Among these many migrants were always some who never left their College from year to year. The Bursar at St Catharine's (Cambridge) took his daily walk in the Grove, just over the river. He had never been known to travel further than Senate House, except on the one occasion, during a long vacation, when the Master persuaded him to walk half way to Grantchester. The scout's job, tied as it was to resident dons and College duties, became a real burden. One Corpus scout reported an elderly don in the 1930s who breakfasted and dined every day throughout the year, seven days a week; because of a disagreement with his colleagues he never dined in Hall. He had the grace to leave for a few weeks every year, but 'Christmas Day, Boxing Day and all, you had to be there for Dr Priddock'. But it was in any case quite common then, and not unknown now, for the Fellows and Tutors to dine together on Sundays during Term, presided over by the Head of House, while The Queen's College held its most important Feast on Christmas Day.

'I WANT SOME SALT—SALT'

Dons' rooms in College were both lavish and austere. A. E. Housman, at Cambridge, rejected all adornment whether in his dress, his ways, or in the College rooms in which

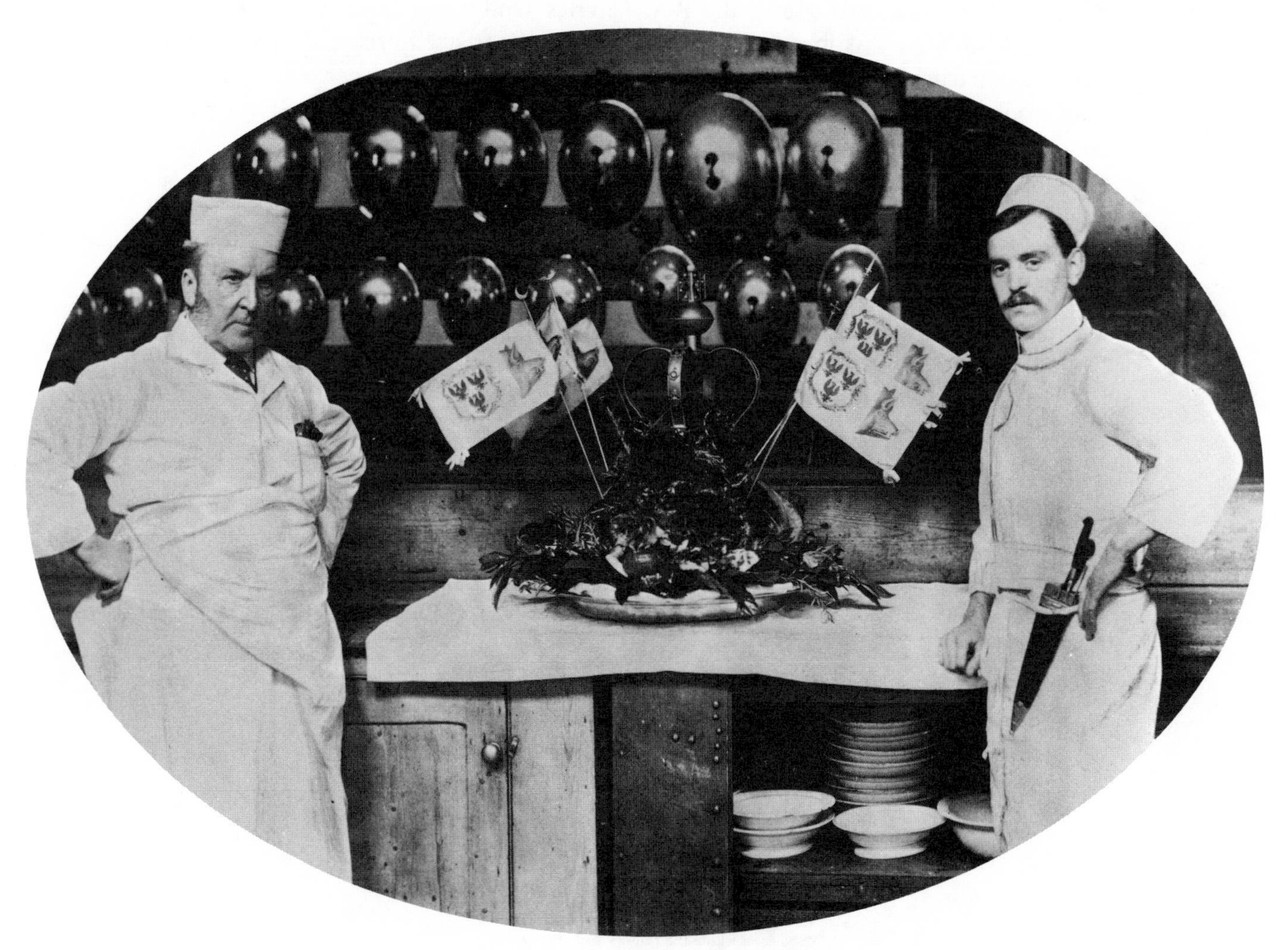

Queen's Christmas Day Feast, 1902

he lived. By contrast, at Oxford, the Rev. Charles Dodgson (Lewis Carroll) had a delightful suite of rooms in a corner of Tom Quad (Christ Church), a paradise for children since from his cupboards came musical boxes, mechanical performing bears, picture books and toys of every description 'in bewildering abundance before the child's astounded eyes'.

Within such rooms scouts coped with almost legendary hospitality. Vere Bayne's ' "little luncheons" and urbane civility/were models of Victorian gentility'. Mark Pattison complained that elderly dons seemed struck with an intellectual palsy, unable to cope with any but the frippery work of attending boards and negotiating phantom legislation; these they followed by giving each other celebratory dinners. Such men, said the embittered Pattison, were the leading personalities of the University, and they set the tone of it – 'a tone as of a lively municipal borough'. In the evenings, dons read Shakespeare plays aloud to each other, and even Pattison had been known to give emotional renderings of 'Rob and his Friends'. F. E. Smith arranged the most lavish and

From the Rake's Progress at the University, by Gilray.

On what dread perils doth the youth adventure,
Who dares within the Fellows' *Bog* to enter.

Laying the table during the vacation at Univ. From ACKERMANN'S OXFORD sumptuous of dinners at which his scout distributed champagne to every guest; champagne was then poured over the ham to get the aroma and all was served with spinach and madeira sauce (F. E.'s favourite dish).

Before the First World War dons often entertained their undergraduates to breakfast – a recognised time for such get-togethers for which a formidable meal was supplied by the College kitchen and served by the scouts: fillets of sole or plaice, cutlets and scrambled eggs, toast and tea and four pints of beer. Lavish feeding did not compensate for the stiffness and formality that so often separate teacher and taught. The Bursar mustered his guests. 'Tea?' asked the Bursar: silence – the undergraduates wait, the chaplain 'uneasy but playful':

> *The Olympian countenance works! – 'Oh! The Provost informed me yesterday that Mr MacTurk had called on him and assured him the glass was falling. So I apprehend that we may look for a change in the weather, although of course I would not venture to be very confident.' We assent; Chaplain looks elated at the information.*
>
> (Frederick Harrison, *Autobiographical Memoirs,* 1911)

Such events were not always to be so painful. The efforts of Augustus Austen Leigh and Henry Bradshaw in King's – the 'new dons' described by Sheldon Rothblatt in his *Revolution of the Dons* – showed their determination to revive the intimacy of a collegiate university: conversation and free access at all times, interest in undergraduate sport and athletics, parties, teas and dinners designed to introduce juniors and seniors. In Oxford in the 1930s choice undergraduates were asked to tea at intellectual houses in North Oxford, at the Haldanes' 'Cherwell Edge', or at 'Yatscombe', home of the Murrays on Boar's Hill. And then, when all else failed, there was sherry, Oxford sherry of abominable quality and served in tiny glasses. Benjamin Jowett, on reading Tennyson's latest poem, felt moved to tell him that if he were himself Poet Laureate he would not

Victorian splendour at Norham Manor, north Oxford

publish it. 'Well, if it comes to that, Master,' said Tennyson, 'the sherry you gave us at lunch was beastly.'

Yet for all its hardships, life was more comfortable in College than it was in the great country house. Augustus Hare, who had experience of both, had been staying at Welbeck, where all was 'vast, splendid and utterly comfortless'; he could imagine no more awful and ghastly fate than waking up one morning and finding oneself Duke of Portland. Servants at Crewe Hall were instructed that no fires were to be lit except between 1 December and 1 May, whatever the weather.

It was the traditional role of the Heads of Houses to entertain the members of their Foundations, senior and junior. Heads had been permitted to marry, by Act of Parliament, from the late eighteenth century, and they were supplied by their grateful colleges with palatial 'Lodgings' and a host of servants. The Spooners at New College entertained in great splendour – elaborate flowers, high silver mugs and tankards, silver dishes, candlesticks and salt cellars; maidservants in dark dresses with black ties, white caps and collars; soup, fish, game, omelettes, dessert and fruit followed by coffee in the Drawing Room. The Rev. Dr Spooner's oddities always surpassed the 'Spoonerisms' for which he is best known, like the time, at dinner, when he poured wine on spilt salt, or the other when, meeting a young Fellow in the Front Quad, he asked him to join a dinner that night to meet Stanley Casson, a new Fellow. 'I *am* Stanley Casson,' said the young man. 'Never mind,' said the Warden, 'come all the same.'

Mark Pattison, as Rector of Lincoln, felt the same duty to entertain, and he invited his undergraduates to Sunday breakfast. It was seldom a happy experience, and he was described (by one of his undergraduates) as:

Irresistibly, I fear,
Suggesting the idea
Of a discontented lizard with a cold.

Eminent Victorians: Dr Wood, Dr Benjamin Jowett and Sir Henry Acland (left). Balliol dons in deep discussion. Robert Nettleship was famed for evading the positive: his nearest approach was when he remarked "not but it may not be; possibly it is" (right)

Chaos in Canon Jenkinns' room at Christ Church, 1955

The Master of Balliol, Benjamin Jowett, was pathologically shy. Nevertheless he asked his undergraduates regularly to breakfast, and enjoyed snubbing the more harmless and well-meaning. The few words that Jowett let out at those solitary and almost silent breakfasts appeared in what E. F. Benson has described as his 'penetrating little weary voice'. Balliol undergraduates liked to provoke gems of Jowettry, and one took courage and remarked, amidst the silence, that it was a fine day. Jowett said nothing until the breakfast was over and his guest rose to go – then: 'That was a foolish observation of yours . . .' after which a new Jowettry was added to the College collection. F. E. Smith was the only person who seems to have been able to stand up to Jowett's silences. He and the Master went for one of those long Oxford walks together. They said not a word until even Jowett could keep silent no longer: 'They tell me you're clever, Smith, are you?' 'Yes,' said Smith and was silent again. No more words were exchanged between them until they reached the College gate. F.E. then paused, held out his hand, and wished the Master good day: 'I've so much enjoyed our talk.'

The relationship between dons and their undergraduates was entirely a matter of personality. Some dons, like M. R. James (Provost of King's), were brilliant hosts, others stilted and laboured, while others, like Dr William Whewell (Master of Trinity), were justly described as 'radiating repulsion'. But in any case Heads of Houses regularly dined among themselves. They 'formed a class apart, exchanging solemn dinners and consuming vasty deeps of port'. Margaret Jeune's diaries for 1843–62 recounted how, as wife of the Master of Pembroke, she had dined with other Heads of Houses, sometimes ponderously but at others in great style with music in the New Gallery at Christ Church. Maurice Bowra, Warden of Wadham, was immensely generous with his hospitality and enjoyed it thoroughly, although he once claimed to be 'more dined against than dining'.

Long servers at Trinity in the 1970s. At the back is Bill Sloper, who started as underboy in 1943 working on Richard Cadman's staircase, and still works as head scout

Chapter 9

AUTRES TEMPS, AUTRES MOEURS

In the last decades of Queen Victoria domestic service was still an expanding area of employment; the 1901 census recorded no fewer than 1.7 million female servants and 140,000 male, and together they constituted by far the largest occupational group in the nation. Yet while the demand for servants' services increased with the prosperity and comforts of the Victorians, fewer men and women were needed to fulfil them as methods and conditions improved.

Running water on 'staircases' was first introduced in Corpus in 1928; previously all water had had to be taken from a tap in the kitchen quad. Even then there were dons in the Fellow's Building who continued to demand that water should be brought to them in the old way, up the stairs to hip baths before open fires, with the water boiled in a kettle below. One of these 'Victorian' dons used to put a white board outside his room for the scout, to show his disapproval if his water had failed to arrive by 7 a.m.

It was the scout's duty to carry up the water, and then to take it away and clear up the mess. John Burnett has explained (*Useful Toil*, 1974) how in private domestic service, gas and electricity (both for heat and light), piped hot water, even the arrival of the telephone, made the task of the male servant easier and therefore less necessary. Proprietary polishes for floors, furniture and silver did not exist for much of the nineteenth century and vacuum cleaners made their appearance only with the twentieth century. Certainly in Trinity (and possibly in other Colleges too) coal fires were still the heating for undergraduate rooms during the later 1950s. Open fires took a heavy toll of a scout's time. Not only did he carry up coal, clear the ashes, re-lay the fires and keep

High table at Pembroke, 1966 — some of the old traditions survive

them burning; the coal brought dirt to the rooms and dust to the wooden stairs, open as they were to the quad: 'Oh yes, so much easier, you don't realise it . . .', said a scout once gas fires were installed; ashbins and mess were to be found in the front quad (Corpus), 'and along came those lovely shire horses . . . all that dust . . .'.

Oil lamps, serviced by scouts, needed daily trimming, cleaning and refilling. Queen's was still using oil at the turn of the century, and it was a porter's duty to go round during dinner and deliver fines to those members whose lamps were left burning. Gas lighting, although introduced in Lincoln as early as the 1850s, was long restricted to the staircases, while oil lamps were retained in the rooms. Hertford was the first College to introduce electric lighting, although by 1905 all others except Keble had done the same. A senior member of Corpus, one of the last of the Colleges to change, was heard to say that he had never known anyone who had once been washed in the electric light who went back to wallow in the mire of paraffin. A scout who had joined University College as a boy in 1904 remembered that one of his first duties both in the early morning and again at dusk was to turn on the master-tap at the bottom of the staircase: 'My word, how you had to fly to get a light to the flares up the stairs as gas rushed out.'

Change at Oxford has always taken time. *Quieta non movere* was the guiding principle of all Bursars. A Bursar's memorandum as recently as 1968 put the bold and innovatory proposal that undergraduates should be asked to make their own beds; this would reduce the domestic staff by two 'part-time women', and save £400/500 a year. The Bursar was uncertain what the Governing Body would make of such an innovation, although he believed that it was already the practice in most, if not all universities other than Oxford and Cambridge. As for self-service at lunch, this might be well enough, 'But do we really want self-service at dinner? at High Table? in the Common Room?'

In a university of so many independent Colleges, often eccentrically managed, shared dates for reform and change are always elusive. Perhaps it is only the antiquarians who care one way or the other: as Robert Browning once said of the poet Austin Dobson: 'Well, some people like carved cherrystones.' It may be true that Oxford changed more as a result of the Second World War than of the First, although there are those who argue the reverse. All that is certain is that it changed, and that for the scouts it changed beyond recognition.

Cambridge, during the First World War, sank to a low ebb; it barely existed. At Oxford, Gervas Huxley told Sybille Bedford, 'one enlisted at once; we all did; we just disappeared'. Nobody, in Trinity Term, 1914, gave a thought to war; by Michaelmas everyone had gone. Aldous Huxley's appalling eyesight kept him at Oxford, away from the Front. He spoke of the 'quiet life of Anglo-Saxon lectures and a crowd of painful young women': 'Frou-Frouery and faint patchouli smells,/And debile virgins talking Keats.'

Exeter, a college of 150 men, was left with only seven in residence – three Indians, two Americans, a Norwegian and a Swiss. About one in three of those who saw active service never returned. In All Souls, where eight junior Fellows had been killed in action, the change was more remarkable than most since the large election of war veterans in November 1919 meant, in Sir Charles Oman's words, that 'the whole of our Ancient Victorian practices [the Bursar's Dinner and its 'sacred games', all very jolly and manly] dropped of themselves'.

Yet the effect on Oxford life in general may not, overall, have been so dramatic. Numbers were back almost to normal by the summer term of 1919, and those who had been up at Oxford just before the War returned zealous in their efforts to restore the old conventions; the new men were only too happy to see them do so. Mark Pattison may have been right that it was Jowett who had been responsible for turning Oxford into a super public school, with competitive games, juvenilia, robust faith and contempt for real scholarship: 'the separation between Jowett and myself consists in a difference upon the fundamental question of university politics – viz., Science and Learning v. School Keeping'. Jowettry survived the Great War, and the University's statutes and regulations still included antediluvian survivals like Pass Mods, described by Aldous Huxley as 'an infernally stupid exam, trod out by the feet of weeping boys from the wine-press of boredom'. The young Keynes soon after he came up to Cambridge at the

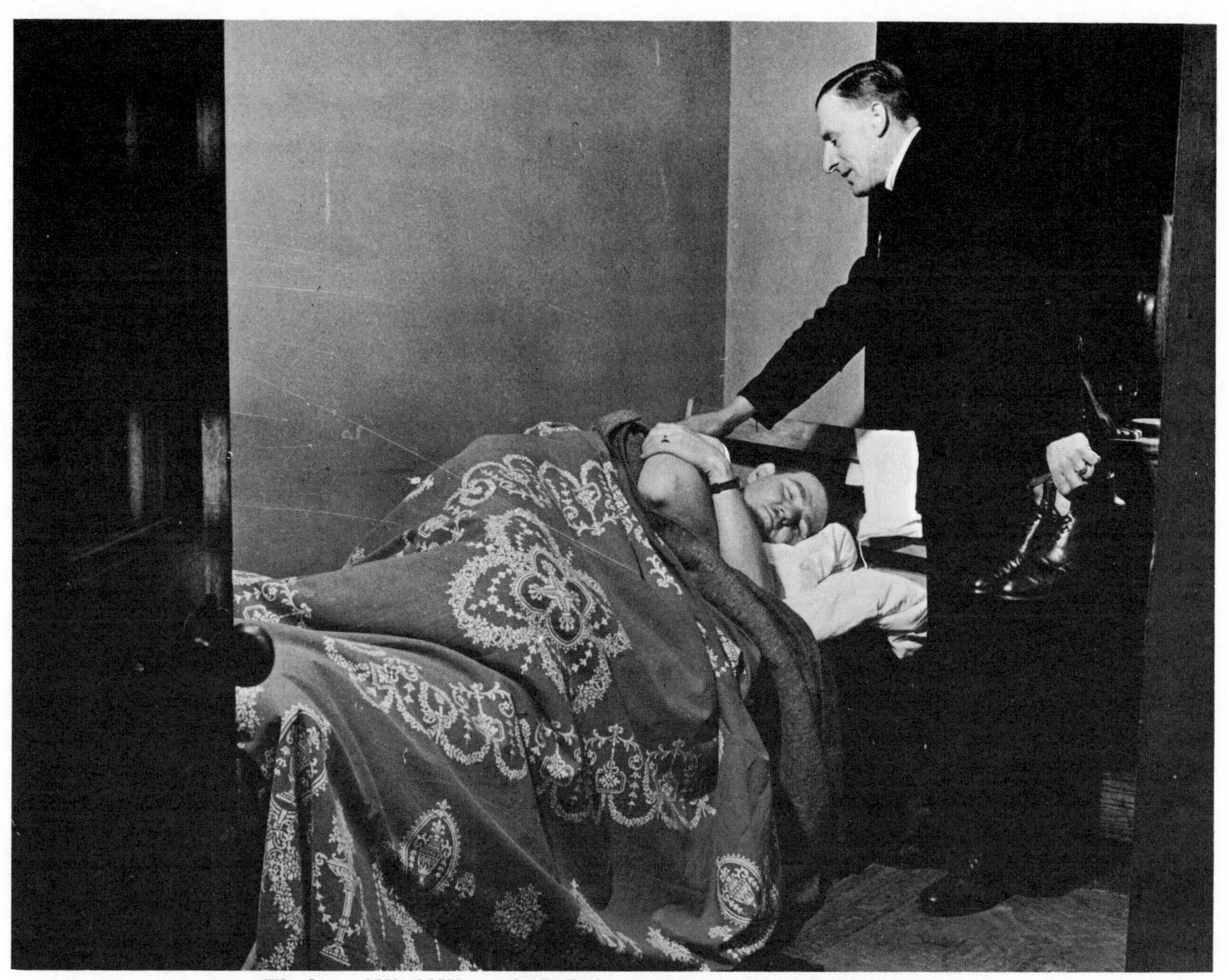

The Second World War and a Balliol scout wakes a brawny American airman

beginning of the century, told the eminent C. R. Fay that by now he had had a good look around the place and had come to the conclusion that it was pretty inefficient. Yet much of what he saw survived 1914–18.

Goronwy Rees dated those changes that were genuinely to affect the social basis of Oxford from the Crash of 1929 and the subsequent Depression. The Left, he argued, may not have had much success in changing the world, 'but [it] certainly transformed Oxford out of all recognition'. This was perhaps the point at which confidence (among Britons) in the continuation of a privileged society was finally destroyed; it had been shaken by the French Revolution and then again by the First World War, but the recovery of the 1920s had seemed to deny it and it would have taken a wise man to have realised the extent of what had really happened. The amazing thing, one don was to say, was how little seemed permanently lost; there had remained a thin thread of continuity, supplied not merely by the more senior dons 'but also – and perhaps more potently – by the elderly scouts and other college servants, that most tradition-steeped and fiercely conservative and loyal body of retainers'. But his book was published in 1925. . . .

None the less it is probable that if the thirties meant more for change in the Oxford of dons and undergraduates, it was the Second World War that transformed College service. Before the War, one scout explained, he was still at work collecting tea trays, building coal fires, drawing curtains; while he and his young men were in Hall, a 'part-time woman' went round the bedrooms, turned down the beds and laid out the pyjamas – indeed, 'different from what it is today'. Things were so quiet in old Oxford – a country market town, a small cathedral city. By the time undergraduates came back from the Second World War some had been majors and colonels and had never been in College; 'Jimmie Jameson', the Bursar of Corpus, found that one of the new undergraduates had been his colonel. The same was experienced, of course, after the First World War, but what had changed was Beveridge and Social Welfare, Butler's Education Act, and a Labour Government; this was what really meant something to the working man. Another quite simple reform was brought about by war and post-war food rationing.

The last generation of college servants: men and *women at Pembroke, 1967*

From now all meals were taken in Hall and breakfasts and lunches were no longer supplied in college rooms: sugar, butter and jam were issued to each man and brought by them to a common meal. When rationing ended Hall meals survived. It was a small thing, perhaps, but it meant much to a scout's timetable.

After the Second World War, the young gentlemen were anyway so different; no longer were they confident grandees drawing on cheap and abundant credit. Fred Bickerton, whose experiences as a College servant spanned the inter-war years, remembered the story of the undergraduate who wondered whether he should give his guests punch or champagne; inevitably he chose champagne because he could find no shop to sell him lemons on account.

So much indeed has changed, and mainly for the better. The dons (most) are better educated; the undergraduates (some) are more industrious; the Colleges are equal opportunity employers, pay proper wages and are managed (occasionally) by professionals. But the scouts are no more, and much of old Oxford has gone with them. For what we have received, may the Lord make us truly thankful.

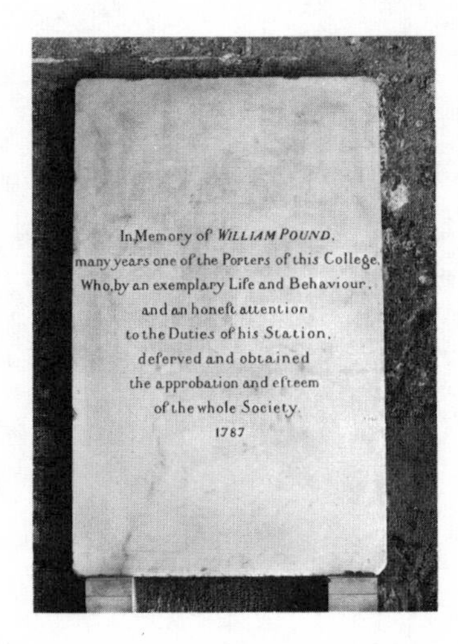

ACKNOWLEDGEMENTS

This is a part of the story of Oxford. Many of us have shared in it, but it is now lost. *Mutato nomine de me/Fabula narratur* (with change of name it is of me the story is told).

I have tried to recreate the life and times of the College scout and I have explained why, except in name, the post can hardly any longer be said to exist. Furthermore, I have done so while an opportunity remains to gather some personal recollections, and my book contains the voices of many who have passed their lives in College service. I owe much to those scouts whom I have interviewed in recent years, particularly to Fred Wheatley, to Alec Lyne and to David Pomeroy, and to others whose memories were recorded more than a decade ago by Brian Harrison and his undergraduates. To these and to Dr Harrison, Senior Tutor of Corpus Christi, I am immensely grateful, as I am so particularly to Fred Wheatley, fine scout, humorist, man of wisdom, taste and discernment. He was Steward of my College when I was a graduate student and he remained so, utterly unchanged, for the decade and more that it took me to return. To the memory of Fred, who died only recently, I dedicate this book.

Many others have helped me, like Professor John Burnett (Brunel University), Dr David Vincent (University of Keele) and Professor Arthur J. Engel (Virginia Commonwealth University). I must say how very grateful I am to my friends at Oxford, particularly to Dr Roger Highfield and to Mr Tom Braun (both Fellows of Merton) and to Professor Kenneth Kirkwood (Fellow of St Antony's). Above all, I am indebted to my wife Sylvia, a professional in publishing, who has watched over the development of this book (and enjoyed the task).

Miss Charlotte Ward-Perkins has taken efficient charge of my inexpert efforts at picture research.

The publishers would like to thank the following for permission to reproduce illustrations: The Master and Fellows of Balliol College: 4, 97, 106; Bodleian Library, Oxford: 16, 18 (left), 41, 45 (right), 69; British Library: 24, 28, 72, 91; Cambridgeshire Collection, Cambridgeshire Libraries: 18 (right); The Governing Body, Christ Church: 14 (left), 64, 132; The President and Fellows of Corpus Christi College: 76 (both); Mr Norman Dix: 85, 107 (top and bottom left); Sir Claude Hayes: 74 (both), 77, 90; The Principal and Fellows of Hertford College: 48, 83; Sir William Hayter: 20; Imperial War Museum: 29; The Principal and Fellows of Lady Margaret Hall: 32 (photo: Thomas Photos, Oxford); The President and Fellows of Magdalen College: 3, 36, 46, 49, 57, 70, 105; The Warden and Fellows of Merton College: 11, 22 (both); The Warden and Scholars of New College: 17; The Provost and Fellows of Oriel College: 14 (right); Oxfordshire County Libraries: 4, 8, 9, 30, 37, 38, 40 (both), 44, 51, 55, 56, 61, 65, 71, 80, 88, 89, 95, 98, 102, 112, 113, 115, 117, 119, 121 (both), 122; The Governing Body of Pembroke College: 78, 87, 94, 126 (both), 131; Mr Harold Prescott: 107 (right); The President and Fellows of St John's College: 2; Sanders of Oxford: 19, 45 (left), 54; Mr Bill Sloper: 109, 124; K. W. Swift, Bookseller: 27, 31 (left), 47, 63, 92; Mr Walter Thomas: 134; The President and Fellows of Trinity College: viii; Mrs Fred Wheatley: ii.

Photography by Michael Dudley and John Peacock, Oxford.

Walter Thomas, head porter extraordinary

107 Kingston Road
Oxford.
Phone 54380 June 5 - 1984

My Dear Professor
as a very old scout for 63 years I must write to you I have done 3 early morning talks on radio Oxford (Mr Ron Tandy) I am getting a bit old now 93 after serving for 3 years in the old Royal Flying Corps I was appointed for a scouts job at Queens College. but after a few years I got the head porters position at all Souls your Warden Mr Carr from ST Anthonys also Mr Pease I was his scout they would remember me. I had to retire from all Souls at 70 age limit I got a very nice job at the Taylorian Library, there was a very interesting television programme on the Midland called Return to Oxford a year or so ago lots of the dons were very pleased they said I was very good. I hope your book will be a success,
Sir Arthur Bryant was always after me to write a book, I was his scout at Queens he has gone now but he was a very nice man to work for

Good luck Professor
Your Very Truly

Walter Thomas

(TOM)